The European Union
A Beginner's Guide

"A well focused introduction to both the history and institutional set-up of the EU. A near-perfect equilibrium between fundamental perspectives and factual detail."

Jörg Monar – Professor of Contemporary European Studies, University of Sussex, and Marie Curie Chair of Excellence, Université Robert Schuman de Strasbourg

"Excellent and very informed."

Finn Laursen – Professor and Canada Research Chair in European Union Studies, Dalhousie University

ONEWORLD BEGINNER'S GUIDES combine an original, inventive, and engaging approach with expert analysis on subjects ranging from art and history to religion and politics, and everything in between. Innovative and affordable, books in the series are perfect for anyone curious about the way the world works and the big ideas of our time.

aesthetics
africa
anarchism
aquinas
art
artificial intelligence
the bahai faith
the beat generation
biodiversity
bioterror & biowarfare
the brain
british politics
the buddha
cancer
censorship
christianity
civil liberties
classical music
climate change
cloning
cold war
conservation
crimes against humanity
criminal psychology
critical thinking
daoism
democracy
descartes
dyslexia
energy
engineering
the enlightenment
epistemology
evolution
evolutionary psychology
existentialism
fair trade
feminism
forensic science
french literature
french revolution
genetics
global terrorism
hinduism
history of science
humanism
huxley

islamic philosophy
journalism
judaism
lacan
life in the universe
literary theory
machiavelli
mafia & organized crime
magic
marx
medieval philosophy
middle east
NATO
nietzsche
the northern ireland conflict
oil
opera
the palestine–israeli conflict
paul
philosophy of mind
philosophy of religion
philosophy of science
planet earth
postmodernism
psychology
quantum physics
the qur'an
racism
renaissance art
shakespeare
the small arms trade
the torah
sufism
volcanoes

The European Union

A Beginner's Guide

Alasdair Blair

ONEWORLD

A Oneworld Paperback Original

Published by Oneworld Publications 2012

ISBN 978-1-85168-898-2
eBook ISBN 978-1-78074-091-1

Typeset by Cenveo Publisher Services, Bangalore, India
Cover design by vaguelymemorable.com
Printed and bound in Great Britain by
TJ International, Padstow Cornwall

Oneworld Publications
185 Banbury Road
Oxford OX2 7AR
UK

Learn more about Oneworld. Join our mailing list to
find out about our latest titles and special offers at:
www.oneworld-publications.com

Contents

Preface

For more years than I can remember I have been fascinated with the study of Politics and International Relations, particularly the relationship between Britain and the European Union (EU). During that time I have been fortunate to discuss my thoughts with staff and undergraduate and postgraduate students in the universities in which I have been employed: the University of Leicester, the Open University, London Metropolitan University, Nottingham Trent University, Loughborough University, Coventry University, and finally De Montfort University. My first words of gratitude are to the colleagues and students who took time to ask questions and raise comments that helped refine my thoughts.

A book of this nature inevitably draws on the labour of many scholars working in the area of European integration. I have been extremely fortunate to have developed a career at a time of great expansion in the literature devoted to the study of the EU. The task of this book is to provide a broad survey of the field and to introduce students and the general reader to the subject matter in an accessible way. This is no easy assignment for a subject such as the EU, which is dominated by turgid language on sovereignty, policy making and inter-institutional bargaining. This book has concentrated on reviewing the key moments in the history of European integration, examining the shifting balances of power between the four main EU institutions, and analysing core EU policies. Many more words could have been invested in looking at other institutions, policies, theories and historical coverage.

The EU is a subject that specialises in producing abbreviations, which can create a degree of confusion. The Treaties
of Rome created two communities: a European Economic
Community (EEC) and a European Atomic Energy Community
(Euratom). In 1967 they merged with the European Coal and
Steel Community (ECSC) to form a single institutional structure. From the 1970s onwards it was commonplace to refer to all
three institutions as the European Community (EC). In the 1993
Treaty of Maastricht the EC became the EU and as such it is
common for people to refer to the EU in recent years, but for the
period prior to the 1990s to use a mixture of EC and EEC. This
is a convention that I have stuck to in this book, although I have
also used the more general practice of referring to the EEC/EC/
EU as simply 'Europe'. This is because 'Europe' is the term that is
often used in debates on the subject.

In writing this book I would like to thank Mike Harpley for
suggesting that I should undertake this task and for providing
valuable comments on drafts. A number of academic colleagues
require to be singled out for their kind generosity and willingness
to offer guidance, support and encouragement to my career over
the years. Particular thanks go to John Young, Philip Lynch,
Wyn Rees, Jörg Monar, Hans Mackenstein, Michael Newman,
John Leopold, Michael Smith, David Allen, Brian Hocking,
Anthony Forster, Steven Curtis, Philippa Sherrington, Christopher
Goldsmith, Alistair Jones, Alison Statham and Finn Laursen.
Thanks are also due to Katherine, William and my family who
remind me of the importance of family and life beyond work.
It is to them that I dedicate this book.

Alasdair Blair
Thornton

Map

The 27 member states and acceding/applicant countries in 2012

Map

1
What is the European Union?

Why would any country want to be subject to rules and decisions that are taken in an arena they cannot control? Today there are a number of examples throughout the world where countries have joined together to form a common organisation. This can be the result of regional concerns, as in the case of the African Union (AU) or the Association of South-East Asian Nations (ASEAN). In other instances, there might be common concerns that cut across regional boundaries. The most obvious example is the United Nations (UN). With a membership of 193 countries, it represents more or less every country in the world.

The European Union (EU) is different from these organisations. From Beijing to Berlin and Lima to London, the policies and decisions that are taken by the EU are of relevance to governments, businesses and individuals. If you live in any of the twenty-seven EU member states the reality is that approximately half of all the new laws that are implemented in your country with an economic focus will have originated from decisions taken by the EU. Non-EU countries do not escape. Children's toy manufacturers in China have to adhere to strict EU controls on the materials used for production. Computer software manufacturers in the United States of America (US) need to be aware of EU rules on fair competition.

These rules do not just materialise in some miraculous way from the predominantly Brussels-based EU institutions. Governments, companies and individuals undertake lobbying to ensure that their views are taken into consideration. In many instances, expert opinion is needed from these sources. This can vary from an eminent scientist, to the views of pressure groups such as Greenpeace, and from trade unions to multinational corporations (MNCs) such as Microsoft. Thus, while announcements that 'Brussels has decided' might be true, the final outcome will usually have been subject to a great deal of discussion. Member state governments are at the centre of this process. This is through their role in the EU decision-making structures as well as the fact that they are often charged with implementing and monitoring EU decisions.

The need for such EU rules can nevertheless provoke a great deal of questioning. Newspaper headlines in Europe often scream 'get us out of Europe'. In non-EU countries headlines frequently criticise EU trade rules. But we have to remind ourselves that there are often very good reasons why such rules and policies do exist. As the EU is the world's greatest importer and exporter of goods, it is sensible for there to be common standards governing the quality of these goods. Otherwise producers inside and outside the EU could be tempted to produce goods of a lower quality and price. Rules are aimed at protecting consumers as well as attempting to ensure that producers face a level playing field. Sometimes the EU does not make the right decisions. EU policies can be too wide-sweeping in their remit, failing to take fully into consideration the views of all parties. Concerns about the impact of using chemicals in manufacturing industries can result in blanket bans that do not always take into account the fact that the conditions and necessity of use might vary between industries.

At the heart of the EU there is a tension between its need to provide broad standards and the desire of individuals, organisations, companies and governments to seek variance from these standards. This often results in a considerable degree of friction between the local level of the member state and the broader

EU level. Reports from the European Commission, which is the EU institution responsible for overseeing the application of EU policies, regularly highlight variation in the implementation of EU policies among the member states.

For example, some member states, such as Britain, often adopt new EU rules with a greater zest than others, such as Greece, and implement policies at the national level that go beyond what is required from the EU. This process, which is referred to as 'gold-plating', can actually undermine efforts to harmonise policies at an EU level. These refinements to EU policies consequently result in additional costs for citizens and businesses that can put them at a competitive disadvantage when compared with other member states. And while a government may consider that there is a perfectly good reason for these additions, criticism can often be targeted towards the EU rather than the member state government at the time of implementation. In this context, Britain's lack of enthusiasm for many initiatives that deepen European integration belies the tendency for its officials and ministers to be extremely efficient in implementing these policies. Other countries such as Italy and Spain can have a more high profile public commitment to European integration, but can drag their feet when it comes to implementation.

Whatever variances exist, it is evident that EU member states face common challenges, from fighting global terrorism to conducting trade negotiations with the likes of China and America, and from dealing with an ageing population to tackling massive public and private levels of debt. In responding to these challenges it is generally acknowledged that the voice of each of the twenty-seven EU member states is stronger and more influential at a global level when it is presented as an EU viewpoint rather than a national viewpoint. This particularly applies to small member states such as Cyprus, Estonia, Latvia, Lithuania, Luxembourg and Malta. All have small populations and as individual countries do not exercise significant influence at the global level. For example, Luxembourg is geographically roughly the same size as the US state of Rhode Island. By contrast, Germany, France, Italy, Poland, Spain and Britain are more influential countries that are able to exercise influence at the global level. But even the largest of the EU member states, Germany, is dwarfed by China, both on economic and population comparisons. Germany's population of approximately 82 million people is less than a tenth of China's one billion. And even if you add the population of all the EU member states together it is noticeable that they are still dwarfed by the likes of China and India.

Frustrations of membership

Within the EU there continues to be much debate among populations as to whether their country would be better off outside the EU. It is a discussion that is not just the preserve of the large member states that are capable of exercising significant global influence by virtue of the size of their economies and the reach of their political power. Indeed, one of the most striking factors is that many small member states have significant sections of their population who also think that their country would be better off outside the EU, given that EU rules often limit the ability for decisions to be taken at the national level.

One of the reasons why such frustrations exist is that the EU requires member states to compromise in order to achieve consensus at the European level. This inevitably means that not everyone gets what they want, with member state governments often having to implement policies that they are opposed to. This was without doubt a less complicated process when the EU was founded in the 1950s with just six member states and when the viewpoints of the governments and peoples of these member states were relatively similar. Today the sheer size of

Enlarging the European Union

Year	Member states	Number of member states
1957	Belgium, France, West Germany, Italy, Luxembourg, Netherlands	6
1973	Britain, Denmark, Ireland	9
1981	Greece	10
1986	Portugal, Spain	12
1995	Austria, Finland, Sweden	15
2004	Cyprus, Czech Republic, Estonia, Hungary, Latvia, Lithuania, Malta, Poland, Slovakia, Slovenia	25
2007	Bulgaria, Romania	27
Acceding country (2013)	Croatia (expected to join on 1 July 2013)	28
Applicant countries	Iceland, Former Yugoslav Republic of Macedonia, Montenegro, Serbia, Turkey	
Potential applicant countries	Albania, Bosnia-Herzegovina, Kosovo	

Note: On 3 October 1990 Germany was reunified as a result of East Germany joining West Germany. Although this was technically not an enlargement of the EU in the context of adding a member state, it was nevertheless a process of EU enlargement.

the EU inevitably means that reaching a compromise is a more complex matter.

On joining the EU all member states agree to decisions in certain policy areas being taken at an EU level rather than at a national level. EU membership also requires countries to make reforms to their economic and political structures to ensure that they are 'fit' to join. This has proved to be a challenge for poorer and less developed countries. The accession of ten new member states from post-Communist Europe to the EU in 2004 and 2007 has been particularly challenging because the cost of economic reforms, such as opening up sectors of the economy to foreign competition and removing government financial support to businesses, has come at a time of constraints on the EU budget. This has meant that there has been less EU financial support available to assist the smoothing out of these economic difficulties, which has often resulted in higher levels of unemployment. An inevitable consequence of this has been that the governments of these countries have faced higher levels of scepticism from their populations about the benefits of EU membership.

A loss of national control is regularly criticised by those who oppose the EU. Eurosceptics argue that the EU interferes too much with the national way of life in the member states. Many Eurosceptics even go as far as to make the case for withdrawal. And while on balance most commentators suggest that the benefits of EU membership outweigh any potential costs, that is not to say that the EU is without its critics. For example, the 2008 financial crisis that has so severely affected the global economy led many people to reappraise the extent to which EU membership and in particular the euro as the single currency is of benefit to their own nation.

The financial crisis exposed a fundamental problem with the euro in that it was not directly linked to the collection of taxes in the member states. This created a vacuum that resulted in a crisis of EU leadership, whereby the European Central Bank (ECB), which controls the single currency, turned towards the decisions of the central banks and governments of EU member states to set national policies to control economic policy, while national governments looked to the ECB to provide economic stability.

If we rewind to the launch of the euro as an electronic currency on 1 January 1999 (it became legal tender on 1 January 2002), at that time it was evident that some EU member states considered that the euro offered a panacea for what had other otherwise been volatile or weak national currencies. This was certainly the view taken by Portugal, Ireland, Italy, Greece and Spain. But it could be argued that rather than providing a beacon of stability, the euro has locked these countries into an economic policy that is not controlled at a national level.

The end result was that the governments of these countries were positioned between the proverbial rock and a hard place. On the one hand they hankered after a return to their own currency, giving them the ability to control economic policy at a national level, such as the setting of interest rates. On the other hand, they recognised that any departure would be a formal sign of weakness that would in turn lead to greater instability at a national level as investors flee to safe havens in other countries. Governments in Athens and Dublin have been faced with a double-edged sword scenario. They seemed unable to ditch the euro because the cost of breaking up would be enormous and yet staying in the euro meant that they had to swallow significant doses of EU medicine to stabilise their economy. Therein lies the dilemma of membership of the eurozone.

What would happen if a country decided to leave the EU? Technically Greenland is the only country that has left the EU when it gained independence from Denmark in 1982. When this happened it was hardly earth-shattering news. Greenland was an overseas territory of Denmark and as such was not a member state. But it would be an altogether different matter if one of the twenty-seven member states were to leave the EU. Back in 1975 the British Labour government led by Prime Minister Harold Wilson held a national referendum on Britain being a member of what was then known as the European Economic Community (EEC). This was a calculated move by Wilson,

who wanted to silence divisions on Europe among his government as well as among the electorate. When the electorate spoke,
67% voted in favour of membership. But the issue of Britain's
membership was not resolved and to this day there continues to
be a strong undercurrent of opposition to the EU.

It would be fanciful to think that the likes of Britain, France,
Germany or any other EU member state would be able to act in
a carefree manner if it left the EU. All of these countries would
still be affected by EU policies and would have to trade with the
remaining member states. But they would trade at a competitive
disadvantage. Their goods and services would be subject to
import taxes. Thus, while withdrawal might create a sense of
greater national identity and lead to a view that sovereignty has
been restored to the nation state, such countries would still be
influenced and shaped by EU rules without actually being able
to exert any influence on them.

In evaluating the reason why twenty-seven European governments have decided to give up whole chunks of their sovereignty to become EU member states, one of the most regularly
cited points is that membership is equated with peace and security. This is a view that is rooted in the horrors of the Second
World War, which claimed over 60 million lives, two-thirds of
which were civilians. After the war countries such as France and
Germany decided to work together to end the national conflicts
that resulted in two world wars.

One of the most basic points is that the EU provides a mechanism to unite the peoples of Europe. Today it is just as common
for British citizens to go on holiday to France and Spain as it is
for them to spend leisure time in their own country. People regularly commute for work-related meetings in other European
countries. Many of the companies that people work for operate
on a pan-European basis. University students are able to study in
other European countries.

REGIONAL INTEGRATION

Regional integration refers to the way in which societies have come together to deal with common issues. The most common aspect of regional integration relates to economic issues, particularly the lowering and removal of customs duties between the member states so as to permit trade to move freely among the specific member states. A customs union requires member states to adopt a common position (or what is often referred to as a common external tariff) in relation to trading with non-member states. In some cases regional integration results in the establishment of formal institutions with policy-making and legal responsibilities. This particularly applies in the case of the EU where the member states have taken a conscious decision to come together and give so-called supranational organisations responsibility for decisions and policies. As a result, the member states have given up an element of national sovereignty.

More than a love–hate relationship?

Despite initiatives that allow European citizens to work freely in other European countries, it is not entirely clear whether over half a century of European integration has actually brought about a common sense of identity and purpose among the citizens of Europe. It is particularly interesting to note the differences in attitudes among the European member states. On a regular basis a sample of citizens in all member states is asked a series of questions by Eurobarometer. This is the EU organisation charged with the task of conducting surveys on a wide variety of subjects relating to European integration. Based on a statistical sample of about a thousand people in each country, one of the most basic questions that are asked is whether people consider EU membership to be a 'good thing'. Results published by Eurobarometer in August 2010 show that across all EU member states 49% of the respondents considered membership to be a 'good thing'. This is close to the lowest levels that have been recorded over the previous decade. It is by no means a convincing figure. It also might lead people to think that the rest of the respondents thought EU membership is a 'bad thing'. This would be the wrong conclusion to make. In fact, only 18% of respondents regarded membership as a 'bad thing' in August 2010. This was a 3% increase on the previous year.

A conclusion that can be drawn from these statistics is that there is a trend towards a reduction in the support for EU membership and an increasing scepticism about the benefits of membership. There can be a number of reasons that influence these developments. For example, national media often portrays the EU in a negative context by stressing the way that EU decisions restrict national policies. This portrayal is not helped by the fact that member state governments are all too often unwilling to engage in a debate with their national electorate about the realities of EU membership, which require a degree of compromise among all governments. The end result is that the EU is often considered to erode national identities. It is a factor that has influenced the creation of a so-called 'identikit' Europe. In other words, the member states have been blended into some form of common identity through the creation of EU policies that stretch across their borders.

But while it is certainly true that there has been an expansion in both the reach of EU policies and the depth of their impact on the member states, there continues to be significant national variation between the member states. For example, the exact impact that EU policies have on member states varies depending on the policy concerned. The best way of looking at this is that while the EU Directive on working time affects virtually all workers in every member state, an EU Directive on the loudness of lawnmowers is going to have more limited impact.

Variances between member states are also influenced by national and local identities. In recent years there has been a greater awareness of the need to reflect regional identities within the EU. Many regions now have representative offices to the EU that are based in Brussels. Regional interests are officially represented in the Committee of the Regions. Member states have also been at the forefront of providing a stronger regional voice. In Britain this has been reflected in the granting of devolution powers to Northern Ireland, Scotland and Wales. A growing sense of national identity has been evident at a broader European level. The end of the Cold War resulted in the creation of more sovereign states. The former Yugoslavia fractured into Slovenia, Croatia, Bosnia-Herzegovina, Macedonia, Serbia, Montenegro and Kosovo. In 1993 there took place the so called Velvet Divorce, which saw the division of Czechoslovakia into the Czech and Slovak Republics. This meant that by 2011 Europe had twenty-one more sovereign states than it had in 1990. For the EU the significance of these changes was that they led to a wave of applications for membership.

Over there, not over here

Expansion of EU membership has raised significant questions about what we actually mean when we refer to 'Europe'. As EU membership has grown from six to twenty-seven countries, there is increasingly a lack of clarity as to where the boundaries of membership rest. The EU stretches from Cyprus in the South to Sweden in the North, and from Ireland in the West to Romania in the East. Moreover, subject to the agreement of the existing member states, the EU will expand to 28 members on 1 July 2013 with the accession of Croatia. There are a number of applicant states that are negotiating membership, notably Iceland, the former Yugoslav Republic of Macedonia, Montenegro, Serbia, and Turkey. Other potential applicants include Albania, Bosnia-Herzegovina and Kosovo.

Each applicant has to pass a number of tests to enable them to become members. This includes their ability to implement EU laws, democratic structures of governance and the strength of their economy. But there is no policy that states that each member state has to have a certain economic wealth or that their political institutions have to be of an equal standing. This means that there are huge differences between the member states. To tackle this situation a great deal of money has been spent by the EU to support countries seeking membership as well as those who have become members. The idea behind such strategies has been to improve the standard of living in the poorer member states as part of a policy of harmonisation.

Somewhat inevitably there has been a great deal of debate about whether enlargement is a 'good thing'. This extends to the implications that an increased number of member states brings about for the influence and power of the institutions that govern the EU as well as their relationship with the member states. This has been referred to as the 'widening' versus 'deepening' debate. Put simply, this relates to whether more member states dilute the strength and influence of the institutions that govern the EU.

The Common Fisheries Policy (CFP) is a particularly good example of the practicalities of EU membership. In Britain, fishermen from the South West of England to the North East of Scotland are governed by EU regulations that tell them when, where and what they can fish for. But catching fish is not like harvesting crops. The basic method of the fishing industry is to trawl nets through the sea and wait to find out what appears. More often than not perfectly good fish are thrown to the deep as they are not part of a quota that has been set by Brussels-based officials. Such a crazy outcome has resulted in newspaper stories that stir opposition to the EU among the public. Yet without any regulations there would be nothing to protect fish stocks from relentless fishing that would irreparably damage fish stocks.

EUROMYTHS

Why do many people have a sceptical attitude towards the EU? One answer is the prevalence of euromyths. They range from the bizarre to the ridiculous and most have their roots in the way that policies to establish common standards across the EU have been wrongly interpreted. For example, proposed EU legislation in 2005 to require employers to assess workers who work in the sun all day resulted in newspaper headlines that the EU was banning low-cut tops for females!

A classic euromyth is the story that emerged in the summer of 2006 that EU officials were requiring the spicy snack known as Bombay Mix to be renamed because the Indian city of Bombay had changed its name to Mumbai. Despite the ridiculous nature of this story, it was nonetheless reported as a fact in Britain's leading popular newspaper *The Sun* on 18 July 2006, with a banner headline of 'EU to rename Bombay Mix'. The origins of the plan had nothing to do with the EU and were instead attributable to a fictitious story put forward by a British regional news agency. The significance of all of this was that many people actually thought that the EU could be capable of such a policy. In other words, they had become accustomed to what they regarded as unnecessary EU bureaucracy.

Probably the most famous euromyth of them all was the 'straight banana' story that emerged in 1994. At first glance people might be forgiven for thinking that this story was in the same league as the Bombay Mix headline. Yet despite the bizarre nature of such a proposal, there was an element of truth to the story. European Commission Regulation (EC 2257/94) stipulated that bananas had to be 'free from malformation or abnormal curvature'. This regulation lay in the desire to create common European rules for certain types of fruit and vegetables. In the case of bananas, this meant that Extra Class bananas had to have no defects, Class 1 bananas could have 'slight defects of shape', and that Class 2 bananas could have full 'defects of shape'. You may wonder why there was a need to have such rules. The fruit and vegetable industry lobbied the European Commission so that EU rules could be established that would assist with pan-European trade.

This was considered necessary as otherwise there would be different standards across the EU, resulting in confusion for producers and consumers. Such practical economic arguments did not stop the media having a field day with what was regarded as another daft policy from crazy EU bureaucrats.

Understanding European integration

To understand the EU we need to look at the pressures that have influenced its development. If we take the example of the initial drive towards European integration in the post-1945 era, many people stress the influence of France and Germany. This focuses attention on individual countries, the role of government, and individuals that have been of particular importance. But we also need to consider the role of business groups, trade unions and political movements. Today this list also includes what are commonly known as social movements. These are groups that reflect particular interests in society, such as Greenpeace or Friends of the Earth.

According to the latest evidence, the EU is now the world's largest donor of humanitarian aid. But what exactly does this mean? Is all aid administered by the European Commission? The answer here is that this refers to both the aid provided by the European Commission as well as the aid provided by member states on an individual basis. So in this sense, the term 'EU' refers to the work of the individual governments and the work that the member states have agreed to be conducted at a collective European level. When we refer to the influence of the EU we are noting both the decisions taken by national governments working in tandem at a European level as well as those decisions in specific policy areas where the EU institutions have been given responsibility and power.

These points raise a common concern that is voiced within and outside the EU as to whether the EU is a state. Yet on many other matters, from trade exports and imports to quotas on fishing, the EU acts as one body similar to that of a state. On many other matters the EU member states have different policies, such as on education, and they also retain their own national laws.

While a great deal of attention is attached to the fact that there has been a growth in the power and influence of policy dealt with at a European level by the EU institutions, we also need to be aware of the fact that the EU budget is relatively small when compared to the combined national budgets of all member states. In 2011 it was actually only around 1.23% of the total Gross Domestic Product (GDP) of all the member states of the EU. Staffing numbers are another area of comparison between the EU and the member states. An instructive example is that there are approximately thirty-four thousand people employed by the European Commission. By contrast, Birmingham City Council, which is Britain's largest metropolitan City Council, employs approximately fifty thousand people. The British National Health Service alone employs over one million people. Going further afield the City of New York Police Department employs approximately 34,500 police officers. The value of these comparisons is, of course, limited by the fact that they are not equivalent roles. But what they do illustrate is that as an organisation, it would be wrong to suggest that the EU employs an excessive number of staff.

In seeking a clearer understanding of the EU, this introductory chapter has sought to emphasise the fact that any study of European integration needs to pay attention to a number of factors that range from national governments through to business movements and the EU institutions themselves. The decision to expand the number of policies that are dealt with at a European level has for the most part been the result of the pragmatic decisions of member states themselves. But we also need to be aware of the fact that it would be wrong to view the EU purely through a lens that highlights the relationship between member state governments and the predominantly Brussels-based institutions. The relationship is far more complex. Emphasis needs to be given to the way that local and regional government engage in policy at a European level.

Some academics consider the EU to be a bit like a tiered cake where the different layers reflect the distinct areas of activity: namely the European, national and local levels. What we can conclude from this is that the EU reflects a multi-level body where there are different centres of power. Not all power rests in Brussels.

2

The creation of the European Community

Why have the EU's policies expanded from coal and steel in the early days of integration to security and defence policy today? Is it the result of pressure from within the member states, a response to developments in non-EU countries, or because of the influence of institutions such as the European Commission, which both takes decisions on and is responsible for the majority of the EU's policies? The answers to these questions can be found by examining the historical development of the EU. In reviewing this history, it is noticeable that the EU's expansion of members and growth in policies has not always been a straightforward process. The EU has developed in the manner of a temperamental car: sometimes it has run smoothly, other times it has backfired, and it has always been subject to a great deal of debate as to its worthiness.

Foundations

The two individuals who are recognised as having played a pivotal role in establishing the foundations of European integration are Jean Monnet and Robert Schuman. They are commonly referred to as the founding fathers of Europe. Both argued that the political and economic recovery of the nations of Europe went hand-in-hand with stronger co-operation between the countries. The Second World War had inflicted massive infrastructure damage on European nations that affected houses, factories and roads. The major European cities lay in ruins, carpeted by a blanket of rubble. Many countries found it difficult to feed themselves. Structures of government barely existed and seemed incapable of dealing with the key challenge of rebuilding nations. It was against this background that Monnet and Schuman argued that institutions should be created at a level above the nation state governments to provide glue that would aid stability in the postwar period and also provide a vehicle for dealing with the key challenges that European nations faced. Such institutions were referred to as 'supranational institutions' as they were operating at a level above nation states. As the main economic and military industries in the postwar years were coal and steel, they argued that supranational co-operation should take place in this economic area.

THE FOUNDING FATHERS: ROBERT SCHUMAN AND JEAN MONNET

The two individuals who are recognised as the founding fathers of European integration are Robert Schuman and Jean Monnet. Monnet (1888–1979) was a key figure in the European integration process after 1945, being appointed head of the French Planning Commission. He argued that integration in one sector could spill over into another. This was a view that was taken up by Robert Schuman (1886–1963), who served as French Finance Minister in 1946 and 1947, Prime Minister from 1947 until June 1948, and Foreign Minister from July 1948 until December 1952. As Foreign Minister he proposed on 9 May 1950 that France and Germany should place their coal and steel industries under a common authority. Known as the Schuman Plan, it provided the basis for the establishment of the European Coal and Steel Community (ECSC), which in turn helped provide the momentum for the establishment of the European Economic Community (EEC), of which the first meeting of the Parliamentary Assembly elected him as President. His role in the advancement of European integration was emphasised in 1986 when the European Communities stated that 9 May (the day when he advocated the ECSC) would be referred to as Europe Day.

Arguments for closer association integration led to the creation of the European Coal and Steel Community (ECSC), which comprised the six nations of Belgium, France, Germany, Italy, Luxembourg and the Netherlands and commenced operation in August 1952. These countries would be referred to as simply 'the six'. The purpose of the ECSC was to create a common market for coal and steel that in turn required European institutions to be established for governing purposes. This approach to European integration signalled the start of a process involving the gradual transfer of sovereignty from the member states to the new institutions that had to be established to ensure the smooth workings of the ECSC.

The support for the ECSC in the governments of the six countries was not to be found in Britain. The British government did not want to get caught up in a process that involved decisions being imposed on the participating states. Britain did not want to dilute its sovereign control over such matters. There were notable economic arguments that supported the British position. In the postwar years Britain − in contrast with 'the six' − was a major producer of steel and had little to gain from joining the ECSC. This compared with the other countries who regarded participation in the ECSC to be crucial to their development. These countries were prepared and willing to accept the loss of sovereignty that came from establishing the ECSC and the institutions that were responsible for governing it.

The key institution in the ECSC was the High Authority. It acted as an executive body that took decisions relating to the Community as it had responsibility for the coal and steel production of the member states. The High Authority initially comprised nine representatives. The larger member states of France, Germany and Italy appointed two representatives, while the smaller member states of Belgium, Luxembourg and the Netherlands appointed one representative. This division was to ensure that the interests of the large member states were protected in the Community. In addition to the High Authority, a Council of Ministers comprised a representative from each of the member states to provide a national viewpoint. A Court of Justice was created to provide a body that could resolve differences between member states, while the Common Assembly offered a degree of democratic representation. The ECSC was significant because it was the first attempt to integrate European states into a supranational structure that was distinct from intergovernmental co-operation.

Cold War

Just as the economic and political difficulties that afflicted European nations after 1945 provided a context to European integration, so too did the onset of the Cold War, which resulted in a division of Europe that was caused by the spread of Soviet influence. The Soviet leader Joseph Stalin was keen to establish a zone of influence that would act as a buffer with the West. This meant that the tentacles of Moscow's control encroached on the great European cities of Budapest, Prague and Warsaw, to name but a few. Some countries, such as the Baltic states of Estonia, Latvia and Lithuania, were swallowed whole into the

Soviet Union. Others in Central and Eastern Europe would remain intact, albeit led by puppet governments controlled from Moscow. All would fall under a Soviet blanket of suppression.

It was Winston Churchill, no longer Prime Minister of Britain, who was among the first to stress the menace posed by the spread of Soviet influence. In a speech at Westminster College in Fulton, Missouri on 5 March 1946, Churchill noted that 'From Stettin in the Baltic to Trieste in the Adriatic, an iron curtain has descended across the continent. Behind that line lie all the capitals of the ancient states of Central and Eastern Europe. Warsaw, Berlin, Prague, Vienna, Budapest, Belgrade, Bucharest and Sofia, all these famous cities and the populations around them lie in the Soviet sphere and all are subject in one form or another, not only to Soviet influence but to a very high and increasing measure of control from Moscow.' By uttering the now famous words that an 'iron curtain' had descended across Europe, Churchill was pointing to the fact that a new conflict had emerged between an American-led Western bloc and a Soviet-led Eastern bloc. This translated into a divide between capitalism and Communism.

WINSTON CHURCHILL (1874–1965)

As the UK's most celebrated Prime Minister of the twentieth century, Churchill served as Prime Minister from 1940 to 1945 and 1951 to 1955 (eight years and 240 days in total). After the landslide Labour Party victory in the 1945 general election, he led the Conservative Party in opposition until 1951 when he once again became Prime Minister. In opposition he advocated closer European integration, urging for the construction of a United States of Europe in 1946. Suffering from poor health and frustrated with not being able to tackle adequately the problems facing Britain in the postwar period, he resigned in 1955.

A new term would quickly be coined to reflect this situation: Cold War. This was a 'cold' war because America and the Soviet Union did not enter into direct conflict with each other. Instead, they vied for influence in other regions of the world. America propped up unsavoury dictators in Latin America and attempted to contain Soviet influence by providing financial and military backing to pro-Western groups, particularly in Asia. Elsewhere the Soviet Union supported Communist-leaning governments in Africa, the Middle East and Asia, and was a staunch ally of Cuba.

This vying for influence spread into the international organisations that sprang up in the postwar world. In the United Nations the competing interests of both countries meant that it was difficult for agreements to be reached. And while an additional division emerged between the interests of states located in the North and the South following decolonisation, the key factor that shaped international relations in the post-1945 period was the bipolar division between the Soviet Union and the United States. Both countries vied for influence in the international community as they sought to establish spheres of influence.

From time to time, the populations of the countries that the Soviet Union dominated revolted against the regimes that were imposed and controlled from Moscow. In the end all were crushed by the Soviet Union. One of the most notable uprisings took place in the early months of 1968 when the leader of Czechoslovakia, Alexander Dubček, attempted to allow freedom of expression and economic reform. Moscow's response to what is commonly referred to as the 'Prague Spring' was swift. It invaded and put a stop to his reforms, which were regarded as being sympathetic towards the beliefs of governments in Western Europe. Taking the name of the Soviet leader at the time, Leonid Brezhnev, this view that Moscow had the right to intervene and stop any policies that undermined Communism became known as the Brezhnev Doctrine. But while the years that followed would see the maintenance of a divide between Eastern and Western Europe, there were nevertheless attempts to establish dialogue between the countries on each part of the divide. This was particularly evident during the 1970s when there was a relaxation of the tension between East and West, a period that became known as détente. But despite this warming in relations, the division of Europe would remain in place until the summer of 1989 when the dissolution of the Soviet grip on Central and Eastern Europe began, which would end with the collapse of the Soviet Union in 1991.

COLD WAR

This term refers to the superpower conflict between the United States and the Soviet Union that emerged in the late 1940s until it came to an end with the collapse of the Berlin Wall in 1989 and the break-up of the Soviet Union in 1991. During this period the super-powers did not engage in direct open conflict with each other. What this meant was that the Cold War did not escalate into actual conflict, otherwise known as Hot War. One of the reasons for the lack of direct conflict was the reality of what came to be known as Mutually Assured Destruction (MAD), whereby each superpower had the capability to launch second strike nuclear weapon attacks against each other. In other words, it was not possible for either country to win a nuclear war. But of course to maintain this state of affairs there was a need for relative parity between each super-power in terms of the number of nuclear weapons that they had. The conflicts that did happen during the Cold War tended to be found in Africa, South America and Asia, where the superpowers often supported particular countries. Such conflicts became known as proxy wars, because the superpowers used third countries as substitutes for fighting each other directly.

The end of the Cold War was supposed to herald an era of peace and security. Instead, the years since have been dominated by regional conflicts and the emergence of new security threats such as terrorism and cybercrime. During the Cold War each side knew who the enemy was. But today this is not so. Former CIA Director James Woolsey captured this feeling well when he said that, following the slaying of the Soviet 'dragon', 'we now live in a jungle filled with a bewildering variety of poisonous snakes, and in many ways the dragon was easier to keep track of'. Thus the post-Cold War world appears to be less controllable. There are a greater number of threats and it is not always possible to know who the threats are from. Former US Defence Secretary Donald Rumsfeld referred to these things as 'unknown unknowns' – the threats 'we don't know we don't know' about.

European integration and the early Cold War

A key question was what impact the Cold War would have on the nations of Europe. After the Second World War the two major victorious powers of the West – Britain and America – were reluctant to roll up their sleeves and get strategically involved in European affairs. America was unclear about the nature of the postwar world, being naive about Soviet motivations and the significance of the balance of power until 1947. Britain looked to its Empire to provide the resources and markets to rebuild its economic and political influence. And even though the wartime leader, Winston Churchill, was one of the few politicians who stressed the need for European unity, this did not mean that he was a strong supporter of Britain playing a leading role in Europe. While he spoke of the need to 'build a kind of United States of Europe' in March 1946, his view was similar to the postwar Labour government of Clement Attlee. Churchill would comment, 'We have our own dream and our own task. We are with Europe, but not of it. We are linked, but not comprised. We are interested and associated, but not absorbed.' Britain supported

European integration, but did not see itself as being part of it. Britain still continued to have a global role. It occupied key strategic positions in many areas of the globe such as the Middle East, Asia and Africa. Some people could rightly comment that in every sense Britain was closer to Australia than France.

But Britain's position was far from secure. Its economic strength had been severely reduced by the war. A belief that this could be recovered through Empire failed to take into account the growing pressure for self-determination in many of the colonies. This included India. Not only had the colonies provided the economic backbone for Britain's wealth, but they had also provided much in the way of the military muscle that helped to maintain Britain's position as a global power. Independence reduced Britain's economic position and weakened its ability to be a global power.

This delicate balance became all too apparent in 1947 when India gained independence. In a stroke it eroded British influence in the East. Closer to home, an economically stretched Britain found it impossible to maintain support to Greece when the government in Athens was threatened by the attempts of Communist guerrillas to take power. Whereas the British government publicly took the view that it was on an equal footing with America and the Soviet Union after the war, in every sense it was a 'shoestring superpower' hanging onto power.

In retrospect it could be argued that Britain should have reoriented its foreign policy towards the European arena immediately after the Second World War. This would have enabled it to take a leading role in the development of European integration and established European structures on its own terms. But the British government of the day chose to pursue a global policy, and this view that Britain had significant interests outside the European arena has been a key factor behind the hesitancy of subsequent governments to commit fully to the European integration project.

At the time, however, the vacuum caused by the absence of British leadership in the early postwar years meant that something had to be done. If Greece fell to Communist forces, then it was feared that other countries including Turkey, Iran, and possibly Italy and France would be affected. Italy appeared particularly vulnerable given that it had a well-organised Communist Party. There was real concern that a Communist victory in Greece would produce a 'Mediterranean crisis' with one country after another falling to Communist influence. The only country capable of stopping this 'domino theory' was the United States and on the afternoon of 21 February 1947 the British Ambassador to Washington, Archibald Clark Kerr, informed the American government that because London could no longer shoulder these demands then the responsibility lay at the feet of America.

Up until 1947 American thinking on the postwar world lacked coherence, particularly as to how to handle the Soviet Union. On 12 March 1947 in a speech before a joint session of Congress, US President Harry Truman said, 'I believe it must be the policy of the United States to support free peoples who are resisting subjugation by armed minorities or by outside pressures.' This came to be known as the Truman Doctrine. It signalled the start of a more active US foreign policy that was centred on a policy of containing Soviet influence. In June 1947 America would go further with the Marshall Plan. In a speech at Harvard University on 5 June 1947, US Secretary of State General George Marshall noted, 'The truth of the matter is that Europe's requirements for the next three or four years of foreign food and other essential products – principally from America – are so much greater than her present ability to pay that she must have substantial additional help or face economic, social and political deterioration of a very grave character.' Based on this analysis, he argued, 'It is logical that the United States should do whatever it is able to do to assist in the return of normal economic health in the world, without which there can be no political stability and no assured peace. Our policy is not directed against any country or doctrine but against hunger, poverty, desperation and chaos. Its purpose should be the revival of a working economy in the world so as to permit the emergence of political and social conditions in which free institutions can exist.'

MARSHALL PLAN

In June 1947 the US Secretary of State George Marshall proposed a plan that would aid the rebuilding of European economies in the wake of the Second World War. The plan offered financial aid as well as other forms of assistance to the war-ravaged countries of Western Europe. Between 1948 and 1951 the plan distributed just over $12.5 billion in aid. The US was concerned that the difficult economic conditions in Western Europe could lead to support for Communist parties and stall attempts to recover world trade, which would in turn impact on the US economy. To administer the plan, the Organisation for European Economic Co-operation (OEEC) was created, which in due course was transformed into the Organisation for Economic Co-operation and Development (OECD). The Marshall Plan played an important role in helping to foster the economic and political recovery of Europe, and was of considerable import-ance in promoting the concept of European integration as well as liberalising intra-European trade.

Security was an additional area of concern. On 4 March 1947 Britain and France signed the Treaty of Dunkirk, which offered a mutual security guarantee. One year later this would be super-seded by the signature of the Treaty of Brussels on 17 March 1948. It committed Britain, France, Belgium, Luxembourg and the Netherlands to a system of collective self defence. In April 1949 the security guarantee went transatlantic when Belgium,

Britain, Canada, Denmark, France, Iceland, Italy, Luxembourg, the Netherlands, Norway, Portugal and the United States established the North Atlantic Treaty Organisation (NATO).

In looking back at these developments, it is evident that NATO was the culmination of a growing US commitment between 1945 and 1949. From then on, NATO would be the cornerstone of European security and would be central to the strategic relationship between the US and Western Europe. And when combined with the economic support that had been provided through the Marshall Plan, this represented a broader union that linked the US and Western Europe together in the Cold War conflict that was pitted against the Soviet Union.

Germany and the division of Europe

If Europe was at the forefront of the Cold War conflict, then the city of Berlin was its centre. In the wasteland that had been left behind by the collapse of the Third Reich, the allied powers decided to divide Germany into occupation zones to provide support and stability, being governed by France, America, Britain and the Soviet Union. In a short course of time, Britain, France and America merged their zones to establish what in due course became West Germany in 1949. Division into East and West Germany was mirrored in Berlin. As Berlin lay within East Germany it meant that the city lay at the forefront of the Cold War. The former Soviet leader Nikita Khrushchev would quip that 'Berlin is the testicle of the West' and 'when I want the West to scream, I squeeze on Berlin'. In March 1948 the Soviet Union restricted Western access to the allied controlled zones of Berlin. It became a total blockage by June 1948 as Moscow tried to cut off Berlin's lifeblood by refusing the transportation of goods by road or rail across East Germany. Instead of caving in to Soviet pressure, the West organised a massive airlift that resulted in every necessity, from food to fuel, being flown into the city. This was essential because at the start of the blockade West Berlin only had thirty-five days' worth of food and forty-five days' worth of coal. At the height of the airlift, planes were landing in West Berlin every three minutes. By the time the blockade ended on 12 May 1949, more than two hundred and seventy thousand flights had been made into West Berlin.

The lifting of the blockade did not demonstrate a thaw in Cold War tensions or a reprieve for the people of Berlin. The division split up families. The desire of people in East Germany to enter West Berlin resulted in the Soviet Union creating a formal division through the erection of the Berlin Wall in 1961. If any feature signalled the reality of the Cold War it was the brutal concrete ugliness of the Berlin Wall. The United States offered support for the people of West Berlin and used the Wall as a mechanism for criticising the Soviet Union at the height of the Cold War conflict. In a visit to West Berlin on 26 June 1963 President John F. Kennedy declared, 'I am a Berliner.' Some years later on 12 June 1987, when standing outside the Brandenburg Gate, President Ronald Reagan declaimed, 'General Secretary Gorbachev, if you seek peace, if you seek prosperity for the Soviet Union and Eastern Europe, if you seek liberalisation, come here, to this gate. Mr Gorbachev, open this gate. Mr Gorbachev, tear down this wall.'

The division of Germany, and in particular Berlin, provides a key backdrop when examining the history of European integration. In the early postwar years the economic weakness of West Germany necessitated support from other European countries, as well as from the US. Britain maintained a significant military presence in West Germany in the form of the British Army of the Rhine (BAOR) from 1945 to 1994. Such forces were also necessary because the legacy of the Second World War meant that West Germany was cautious with regard to asserting a significant military presence. This West German constitution (the 'Basic Law') forbade the authorisation of its armed forces to operate outside its own borders.

As West Germany got economically stronger, the legacy of the Second World War meant it was cautious about exerting political influence in the development of Europe. France had the upper hand. Commentators referred to West Germany being an 'economic giant and a political dwarf'. In this sense, the legacy of the Second World War continued to shape the views of policy-makers within and outside the country.

Beyond coal and steel

With the successful establishment of co-operation in the area of coal and steel, momentum began to build up around the idea of extending co-operation into other policy areas. Defence appeared ripe for this challenge. America was keen that West Germany was brought into the European defence fold at a time of Cold War tension. The Soviet Union conducted a successful atomic test in the autumn of 1949 and the Korean War started in 1950. For obvious reasons, restrictions had been placed on West German rearmament after the Second World War. Yet the sheer size of the country meant that it had the potential to offer much to the defence of Western Europe. A solution lay in a plan for a European Defence Community (EDC) that was hatched by the Premier of France, René Pléven, in October 1950. At the centre of the plan was the creation of a supranational European army of some one hundred thousand soldiers. But there was nervousness among governments over German rearmament and the relinquishing of national sovereignty over defence matters to a supranational organisation. France held this view and on 30 August 1954 the French National Assembly rejected the EDC Treaty.

SUPRANATIONALISM

Supranationalism is the level above national governments. Thus, in the EU supranationalism refers to the way in which the member state governments have transferred powers to institutions. Today this includes the European Commission, which combines both an administrative role for managing EU policies and an executive role for taking decisions on these policies. Other institutions include the European Parliament, which acts as the democratic check in the EU through its elected members. The Council of Ministers comprises, as its name suggests, ministerial representatives from the member state governments and acts as a counterbalance to the Commission by reflecting the interests of national governments. A final key institution is the Court of Justice, which provides an independent legal viewpoint. In the EU a great many decisions are taken at the supranational level. In some instances, this results in the European Commission taking decisions independent of the member state governments. In other situations, it can be that the decisions are taken by the member state governments themselves, albeit by a majority vote.

The failure of the EDC Treaty sent a shockwave across 'the six'. It undermined Monnet's 'spillover' view of European integration. This was where the effect of integration in one policy area 'spilled over' into other policy areas. Some people concluded that European integration had reached its limits. Others were more hopeful. The Belgian Foreign Minister, Paul-Henri Spaak, grasped the nettle. He drafted a memorandum that resulted in the Foreign Ministers of 'the six' turning up at the Italian port of Messina in June 1955 with a view to examining proposals for further European integration. This specifically applied to the creation of a common market and atomic energy community. Other countries were invited to participate in the talks.

This included Britain. But after a short time the British government withdrew from the discussions because of a fear over supranational co-operation. Britain's preference for open and free markets went against the plan to create a common market that involved the erection of trade barriers for those countries outside the market. Eventually the talks that had begun at Messina resulted in an agreement on the establishment of a common market and atomic energy community. As both Treaties were signed in Rome on 25 March 1957 they became known as the Treaties of Rome. They were swiftly ratified by the national parliaments of 'the six' and came into effect on 1 January 1958 and in doing so established the European Atomic Energy Community (Euratom) and European Economic Community (EEC).

Securing the foundations

One of the key objectives for the creation of the EEC was the establishment of a common market. To govern the Community the framers of the Treaty of Rome maintained the same design as the coal and steel community. Even the names were more or less the same. The European Commission was charged with administering and putting into effect the policies the member states agreed to. It acted as an executive (like a national government) and an administrative body (like a civil service). To counteract the supranational viewpoint of the Commission, the Treaties ensured that the views of the member states were taken into consideration through the creation of a Council of Ministers. This was a grouping of government ministers whose membership was determined by the subject discussed. Trade Ministers met to discuss trade policy, Agriculture Ministers to discuss agricultural policy and so on. An area where the founding fathers were less clear about – some say deliberately so – was in providing a democratic element to the institutions through the election of directly elected representatives. So instead of this, a Parliamentary Assembly was created whose members were made up of representatives of national parliaments. It was not until 1979 that direct elections were introduced to what had now become known as the European Parliament. Finally, because the Community is a legal body, a Court of Justice was established to interpret the Treaties and decisions that had been taken.

Key policies included establishing a Common Agricultural Policy (CAP). A Customs Union was also established to allow trade to flow freely among the member states. This required removing the national tariff barriers that the member states had put in place to protect their own industries, as well as creating a common external tariff to ensure that any imports from non-EEC member states were subject to the same level of tariff. This objective was basically reached by 1968 with the establishment of a Customs Union. Yet that did not mean that trade in goods could move freely throughout the Community. This was because the member states sought to protect their own industries through what came to be known as non-tariff barriers to trade. In other words, while goods could theoretically move freely across the Community, their passage was often hindered by the fact that one country did not recognise the standards of production of another country.

The establishment of key policies saw the Community take on a stronger external role. As early as 1961 the EEC participated in the Dillon Round of trade negotiations that were part of the General Agreement on Tariffs and Trade (GATT). Most significantly the Community member states adopted a collective position that represented a move away from national stances. The subsequent Kennedy Round of trade negotiations from 1963 to 1966 saw the Community establish a stronger external trade position, which enabled it to resist pressure to adopt policies from other countries, most notably the US.

THE COMMON AGRICULTURAL POLICY

Any study of the history of European integration will emphasise that the CAP has been one of the most important and influential policies. It has also been one of the most wasteful. One of the reasons for this is that it has suffered from entrenched national farming interests that have stopped important reforms taking place. The initial rationale for the CAP was to ensure stability in the supply of agricultural produce. Mindful of the food shortages that existed in Europe after the Second World War, there was a genuine groundswell of opinion that there was a need to ensure adequate food production. Huge numbers of people were also employed in the agricultural sector, accounting for up to 20% of the labour force in some member states. A combination of factors meant that there was a need to provide support to this industry. For this to be achieved, the Commission established a system of guaranteed payments to farmers that rewarded them for maximising production. This inevitably resulted in massive amounts of money being spent to support the work of the CAP, with it accounting for approximately half of all Community expenditure right up until the 1990s. This was despite the fact that improvements in technology meant that fewer and fewer people actually worked in the agricultural sector of the economy as time went by.

The problem of de Gaulle

Tensions between the creation of new policies and institutions at the European level and the desire of member states to maintain national control came to a head in 1965. The President of the Commission, Walter Hallstein, outlined a number of measures that sought to provide a financial basis for the CAP with a requirement that budgetary expenditure should be subject to the approval of the Parliamentary Assembly. This initiative had arisen because Hallstein regarded the existing method of financing the

Community budget out of national contributions to be inadequate. In addition to this issue, member states were concerned about the provision in the Treaty of Rome to make use of majority voting in a number of areas of the work of the Council of Ministers from 1966 onwards. The implication of these developments was clear: they would result in a further erosion of national sovereignty as individual member states could be outvoted on policies that were of particular concern to their national interest.

CHARLES de GAULLE (1890–1970)

Born in Lille on 22 November 1890, Charles de Gaulle embarked on a military career, serving with distinction in the First World War. He spent much of the 1930s arguing that France should not rely on the Maginot Line of concrete fortifications that had been constructed after the First World War to provide a defence against Germany. He advocated greater reliance on the likes of tanks. When Germany invaded France in 1940, de Gaulle, who by this time was the French Undersecretary of Defence, refused to accept France's truce with Germany. Instead, he escaped to London where he took on the role of leader of the Free French. When Paris was liberated in August 1944 de Gaulle returned as a hero and played a crucial role in establishing the Fourth Republic. But his discontent with the lack of a strong Presidency in the Fourth Republic led him to retreat from national politics.

His retirement from office in 1946 through discontent over the Fourth Republic's constitution reduced his influence upon French politics. When the Fourth Republic collapsed in 1958 after a revolt in French-controlled Algeria, de Gaulle returned to lead France as President of the Fifth Republic. He held great sway in establishing a Presidency that had a strong nationalistic focus, paying great attention to ensuring that France was strong both economically and militarily. This led to tension with other countries, such as the United States when he withdrew France from the military structure of NATO. As a result NATO's headquarters were ejected from Paris and had to relocate to Brussels. De Gaulle wanted France to have a dominant influence within the European Community and suspicion of British motives for membership resulted in him twice vetoing applications from London. His period as President came to an end in April 1969 after he lost a referendum on government reforms.

The French President, Charles de Gaulle, reacted furiously to the Commission's proposals. He recalled to Paris his representatives to the Community. As France held the Presidency of the Council of Ministers at that time, this meant that there was in effect a hiatus in the work of the Community. This period became known as the 'empty chair crisis', with the situation only being resolved at a meeting in Luxembourg in January 1966. Commonly referred to as the 'Luxembourg compromise', the agreement stressed that where 'very important interests of one or more partners' were at stake, the member states would seek to achieve a unanimous agreement. In other words, the pendulum had swung away from majority voting.

The significance of this outcome cannot be stressed enough. It emphasised that member states had been successful in asserting their views and it signalled a decline in the influence of the European Commission. The outcome emphasised the influence of France, which under de Gaulle's leadership was the most important member state in the Community. In 1963 and 1967 he vetoed Britain's applications for Community membership. In a statement on 14 January 1963 he said that Britain 'is, in effect, insular, maritime, and linked through its trade, markets and food supply to very diverse and often very distant countries. Its activities are essentially industrial and commercial, and only slightly agricultural. It has, throughout its work, very marked and original customs and traditions. In short, the nature, structure and economic context of England differ profoundly from those of the other States of the Continent.' Stressing his fears about Britain becoming a Trojan Horse for US influence, he would go on to note that 'in the end there would appear a colossal Atlantic Community dependent on the US and under American leadership which would soon completely swallow up the European Community'. Later in 1967 he said that Britain showed a 'lack of interest' in the Common Market and would require a 'radical transformation' before joining the EEC, noting that the 'present Common Market is incompatible with the economy, as it now stands, of Britain'. In retrospect a question that has to be asked is whether de Gaulle was correct to veto the British applications. His argument was that Britain did not see itself as a European power and that its closeness to America meant that it would permit undue American influence on the Community.

The paradox here is that the political stability and economic growth that the Community had begun to enjoy had largely been the product of American influence. Nevertheless, there is some truth in de Gaulle's point of view as successive British governments attached priority to the significance of the so-called special relationship with the United States. There were a whole number of reasons for this, from the sharing of military secrets to the US providing the financial backing that kept Britain functioning. The dilemma for Britain was that, while it required the economic stimulus that Community membership offered, it could not divorce itself from America or the Commonwealth. Consequently political leaders in government did not seek to gain membership at any cost.

3

From European Community to European Union

Given that the 1960s was a decade when a great deal of effort was spent on establishing the framework for the working of the Community, there was a general view among the EU member states that the 1970s would offer an opportunity for a widening in membership and an expansion in the number of policies dealt with at the Community level. The omens seemed good. In the period between 1958 and 1970 trade among the six Community member states increased by some five times. Exports to the rest of the world increased by two and a half times. The Gross Domestic Product of Community member states grew at an annual average of 5%. There was also a queue of countries wanting to join. More significantly de Gaulle's successor as French President, Georges Pompidou, was in favour of enlarging the Community's membership. Pompidou also wanted the Community to make progress with further economic and political integration, championing its so-called 'relaunch' at a special meeting in The Hague in December 1969.

Looking to the future the member states decided to commission two reports to investigate the opportunity for deeper economic and political integration. When the reports were published in 1970, their proposals for economic and monetary union and foreign policy co-operation were ahead of their time. The proposals touched on the raw nerve of national sovereignty and in any case the Community was nowhere near ready to undertake integration in these policy areas.

A more fruitful area of progress concerned the opportunity for enlargement. Negotiations started in June 1970 with the four applicant states of Britain, Denmark, Ireland and Norway. On 1 January 1973 Britain, Denmark and Ireland joined the Community. Norway did not join because domestic concerns over the impact of Community membership on the agricultural industry resulted in the terms of membership being rejected in a popular referendum. The three new member states added 60 million people to the Community, which in 1973 had a combined population of 250 million. This was an amount broadly equivalent to the US population at the time. Enlargement also increased the Community's economic and political influence, with it now accounting for approximately one-fifth of world trade.

The year 1973 was also significant because the US administration of Richard Nixon designated it the 'Year of Europe'. In a speech on 23 April 1973, Henry Kissinger — Nixon's National Security Adviser, who became Secretary of State during the year — called for a 'new Atlantic Charter setting the goals for the future'. While the US was keen to put renewed vigour into the transatlantic relationship after a series of difficulties that included the Vietnam War, the initiative created a number of dilemmas for European politicians. The British government of Edward Heath, which was keen to establish closer links with European states while still maintaining close ties with America, was concerned that the US initiative would renew French concerns that Britain would be an American Trojan horse in Europe. And when France became reluctant to engage in constructive dialogue with the US, Kissinger in turn criticised the British for their failure to secure French support.

1973 – THE YEAR OF EUROPE

The problems in transatlantic relations are real. They have arisen in part because during the fifties and sixties the Atlantic Community organized itself in different ways in the many different dimensions of its common enterprise. In economic relations, the European Community has increasingly stressed its regional personality; the United States, at the same time, must act as part of, and be responsible for, a wider trade and monetary system. We must reconcile these two perspectives. In our collective defense, we are still organized on the principle of unity and integration, but in radically different strategic conditions. The full implications of this change have yet to be faced. Diplomacy is the subject of frequent consultation, but is essentially being conducted by traditional nation states. The United States has global interests and responsibilities. Our European allies have regional interests. These are not necessarily in conflict, but in the new era neither are they automatically identical. In short, we deal with each other regionally and even competitively in economic matters, on an integrated basis in defense, and as national states in diplomacy. When the various collective institutions were rudimentary, the potential inconsistency in their modes of operation was not a problem. But after a generation of evolution and with the new weight and strength of our allies, the various parts of the construction are not always in harmony and sometimes obstruct each other.

Source: Secretary of State, Henry A. Kissinger, Address to the Associated Press Annual Luncheon, New York, 23 April 1973 – 'The Year of Europe'.

Contrary to expectations, the process of enlargement did not result in the Community making further progress towards deepening European integration throughout the 1970s. This was the result of two key factors. The first of these was influenced by the election in Britain of a new Labour government in

February 1974, which committed itself to a renegotiation of the terms of membership, which were then subject to a referendum vote in June 1975. And although in the end membership was supported by approximately two to one voters, the process of tearing up the terms of membership was a profound shock to the Community.

The second was instability in the international economy, which resulted in rising unemployment and high levels of inflation in many industrialised economies. Economic conditions were affected by the October 1973 Arab–Israeli War, which was followed by a 400% rise in the price of crude oil, which in turn created an energy crisis. These external problems meant that the energies of member state governments were focused on lessening their impact within their own countries. At the same time the institutions of the Community appeared to be too weak to deal with the challenges that the Community faced. These events combined to limit the opportunity for progress on such issues as the objective of creating monetary union by 1980. The sluggish progress would be referred to as Eurosclerosis.

The not so perfect common market

There was a hope that as the Community progressed into the 1980s the decade would unleash fresh opportunities for integration. The first signs of this had taken place the year before when the European Parliament had its first ever direct elections in the summer of 1979. Before 1979 representatives to the European Parliament were appointed by national parliaments, as had been the case with the Common Assembly of the European Coal and Steel Community. The process of appointment of representatives was clearly unsatisfactory as it meant that a question mark hung over the European Parliament's independence and consequently its ability to act as a check on the power of other

Community institutions. Even representatives to the European Parliament were unhappy with this situation and after a number of negotiations the member state governments agreed to the holding of direct elections. Not only did this give a new legitimacy to the Community, but it also brought a new sense of energy to the Community's activities. The Community increased its membership to ten with the accession of Greece in 1981, followed by Portugal and Spain in 1986.

In many senses there was a lot to be pleased about. Yet there were also more substantive issues that the Community needed to tackle. This included dealing with a more active US foreign policy after Ronald Reagan assumed the Presidency in 1981. Reagan wanted to overcome the 'Vietnam syndrome', which was the lack of willingness in America for intervention in the developing world, and the 'Carter syndrome', which was a weak stance against the Soviet Union. This would take the form of a renewed Cold War conflict against the Soviet Union as the US advanced a more aggressive foreign policy. Such a position created anxiety among European governments, who were concerned about US willingness to focus on its own national interests without concern about the impact on European governments. This was particularly evident in the economic arena where the US policy of trade sanctions against the Soviet Union was intended to squeeze the Soviet economy so that Moscow would have to choose between guns and butter. But this form of trade war did not sit well with European governments, who were conscious of being dragged into a trade conflict and as a result refused to support the US action.

Uppermost in the attention of European governments was the need to reinvigorate their economies at a time of rapid technological change that had a dramatic and profound impact on society and the economic means of production. Evidence of this revolution was to be found everywhere, from the Sony Walkman to the emergence of microwave ovens for domestic cooking and the rise of the personal computer. The heartbeat of these developments was to be found in America and Japan.

At a time of such dramatic change in the global economy, Europe's leaders spent a lot of time trying to resolve a somewhat archaic and complicated procedure for funding the Community budget. The election of Margaret Thatcher as British Prime Minister in 1979 brought these matters to the fore. She would write in her memoirs that 'In spite of North Sea oil, by 1979 Britain had become one of the least prosperous members of the Community, with only the seventh highest GDP per head of population among the member states. Yet we were expected shortly to become the largest net contributor. So from the first my policy was to seek to limit the damage and distortions caused by the CAP and to bring financial realities to bear on Community spending.'

Britain was certainly justified in its argument that the level of its contributions were out of line given the fact that its wealth was actually less than the Community average. After a number of diplomatic meetings in which Margaret Thatcher harangued her European counterparts, an agreement on the budget was finally achieved at the June 1984 Fontainebleau European Council.

The resolution of the budget question provided the Community with the opportunity to progress towards closer economic and political integration. This included a need to improve its economic fortunes vis-à-vis the US and Japan. There was also a realisation that while a common market had been established as far back as 1968, there still remained considerable obstacles to free trade within the Community. This was because member states undertook policies to protect their own domestic interests. For example, French liquors could not be easily imported into West Germany because they did not meet West German standards. British companies found it difficult to sell services, such as insurance and banking, in other member states. Governments in all the member states tended to provide national companies with unfair competitive advantages through the likes of financial support.

Such strategies had been influenced by the practical realities that their own national – and not European – electorates elect member states' governments. At times of economic strife it was unsurprising that governments would avoid championing European policies if they undermined national causes. This sort of protection of domestic markets meant that many European companies had become uncompetitive when compared to their international rivals.

The governments of EU member states became increasingly aware of the need to tackle these issues, with the domestic political agenda in many European countries at this time favouring free market competition. Business lobby groups also supported change. Concerned about a competitiveness deficit in the Community, the European Commission was prompted into action. It set about designing a programme of measures that would be necessary to create a European single market where products, goods and people could be exchanged without the restriction of national tariff barriers. Led by the British European Commissioner, Lord Arthur Cockfield, the study outlined nearly three hundred separate measures that needed to be undertaken to create what is now known in Europe as the single market.

To enable this change to happen, the member states agreed to set up a negotiating framework that would produce the necessary legislation to make the single market happen. Known as an intergovernmental conference (IGC) negotiation, its purpose was to amend the existing Treaties of Rome. They too had been the product of an IGC negotiation that lasted from 1955 to 1957. The negotiations that took place in 1985 were much shorter and lasted not much more than three months. Although a lot of the work was thrashed out by diplomats, the Foreign Ministers and heads of state and government of the member states took a keen involvement. And it was they who agreed to the final text when it was submitted for approval at the December 1985 Luxembourg European Council.

The Commission's plans became known as the single market programme and these were agreed to by member states in what became known as the Single European Act (SEA) at the Luxembourg meeting. From 1986 to 1992 the Community set about adopting some 280 items of legislation considered essential to prize open national markets. In many instances this resulted in the creation of common EU regulations that ensured that different national rules were replaced by one European rule. In other instances, the member states agreed to recognise each others' laws and technical standards in the same way that they did their own. This came to be known as the principle of mutual recognition. An obvious example of this relates to qualifications, where differing qualification frameworks within member states hindered the free movement of people throughout the Community.

The end result was the establishment of a structure that permitted the free movement of people, goods, services and capital. This became known as the four freedoms. In practical terms, this manifested itself in the ability of people to live, work, study and retire in another member state. Today the vast majority of people take for granted what is referred to as the single market. We think nothing of the ability to travel freely within the borders of the EU. Little thought is given to the practicalities that make it possible for a Polish student to study in France, or for a French electricity company to provide power to homes in Britain. When we withdraw money from a bank, we do not think about what is required for a Spanish bank to operate in Germany. Nor do we consider the factors that enable qualifications to be recognised across all EU member states. This permits the likes of doctors, hairdressers, plumbers and driving instructors to find work and set up businesses in other member states. The mobility of workers is particularly evident in the case of Luxembourg, where approximately half of its three hundred and fifty thousand labour force commute from neighbouring countries such as Belgium, France and Germany. This in itself is hardly surprising given that the total population of Luxembourg is just over half a million people.

On a day-to-day level the single market brought benefits in terms of greater competition that, it is argued, have helped to drive down prices within the Community. Obvious examples of this have been reductions in the price of airline tickets and mobile phones across the EU.

The SEA was the first major revision of the Community since the 1957 Treaty of Rome, with the agreement making a number of important changes that went far beyond the single market focus. This included widening the scope of the Community's activities into new policy areas such as the environment, as well as making changes to the way that decisions are taken through the introduction of majority voting in the Council of Ministers. This would mean that a member state could no longer stop agreement on certain policies if they were against them. Life in the Community would never be the same again.

MEMBER STATE GOVERNMENTS AND EU DECISION MAKING

Member state governments in the early years of the Community took decisions in the Council of Ministers on a unanimity basis. In other words, all governments had to be in agreement, which meant that any one government could veto a decision if it did not like it. Since the introduction of the Single European Act there has been a steady reduction in the use of unanimity and a concurrent rise in qualified majority voting (QMV), whereby each member state is allocated votes relative to the size of their population. The introduction of QMV has been an important means of speeding up the decision-making process that would otherwise have ground to a halt because of differences between member states. The rider to this is, of course, that member state governments are often forced to accept decisions that they find unpalatable. Only the most sensitive of issues remain subject to unanimity, such as social security and taxation.

Implementing the single market

Standing before the European Parliament on 6 July 1988, the then President of the European Commission, Jacques Delors informed the auditors that within ten years he expected that 80% of economic legislation, and perhaps social and taxation legislation, would be of European origin. For many observers this was fanciful stuff. Speaking on BBC radio a week later, Margaret Thatcher would refer to these as 'airy-fairy ideas' and that Delors had 'gone over the top'. Not everyone shared Britain's views. Some could see how the single market programme that was agreed in the Single European Act would have far-reaching ramifications on a whole range of policy sectors.

Nearly a quarter of a century later it is impossible to give a precise response as to whether Delors's prediction has become a reality. If we examine the implementation of single market directives, it is evident that some member states appear to take their responsibilities for implementing EU legislation more seriously than others. In September 2011 the European Commission reported that the worst offender for failure to implement single market directives was the Czech Republic. At the other end of the scale Malta was the best at implementing directives. One of the big issues is that member states are taking longer to implement EU legislation. Such foot dragging means that on average a member state takes an extra 5.5 months to implement an EU Directive after the deadline for transposition has expired. As of 2011,

Austria and Sweden were the member states that had taken the longest to implement a single market directive. They were supposed to have implemented the EU Directive on publicly available electronic communication services and public communication networks by 15 September 2007. Thus, by 2011 over four years had passed since the deadline for implementation.

For the EU, when one or more member states delays the implementation of a directive, this creates a gap in the overall legal framework. In other words, whereas the single market is supposed to cover all member states, the end product can become a patchwork quilt. This can have a negative impact on the economic interests of all member states as the benefits of the directive cannot be applied across the EU. In EU-speak, the statistics that show the gaps that exist in the implementation of directives are referred to as the 'fragmentation factor'. The latest evidence published in 2011 shows that the single market has a fragmentation factor of 6%. What this means is that the single market is only working at 94% of its potential, with ninety directives having not been implemented on time in one or more member state. The areas of the economy worst affected are transport and the environment. A consequence of this tardiness is that the single market is not a reality in a number of key sectors of the economy.

An additional problem is that when directives are implemented, it is sometimes the case that they are implemented wrongly. Where misapplication is evident the European Commission starts infringement proceedings against a member state. This can result in a member state being taken to the European Court of Justice. In May 2010 the European Commission requested Greece to amend its legislation on the minimum prices that lawyers could charge for their services, as it argued that such rules limit the potential for lawyers from other member states to operate in Greece, thereby restricting the range of legal services on offer to Greek citizens. In June 2007 the European Commission referred Belgium to the European Court of Justice because the Belgian government was imposing conditions on employers who wanted to appoint within Belgium non-EU workers who were already working within the EU. Simply put, Belgium was adding an additional tier of rules to protect Belgian workers from the movement of non-EU workers into their country.

To many observers, the actions of member states such as Greece and Belgium appear quite rational given that the first duty of any elected national government is to protect its own citizens. But fundamentally where such actions contravene existing EU laws, the Commission has to respond by asking member states to amend their policies, and if that does not produce a satisfactory response then it brings the matter to the European Court of Justice. And even though member states may feel that they have been harshly treated by such actions, they have agreed to the necessity of these procedures to ensure compliance among all member states. And moreover, member states would have already collectively agreed to the policies under question, albeit via majority voting in the Council of Ministers.

LOST IN TRANSLATION: THE OFFICIAL LANGUAGES OF THE EU

Have you ever wondered how many official languages there are in the EU? With twenty-seven member states the EU has twenty-three official and working languages. They are: Bulgarian, Czech, Danish, Dutch, English, Estonian, Finnish, French, German, Greek, Hungarian, Irish, Italian, Latvian, Lithuanian, Maltese, Polish, Portuguese, Romanian, Slovak, Slovene, Spanish and Swedish. As more countries join the EU other languages will inevitably be added. There are also more than sixty indigenous regional and minority languages in the EU. Many other languages are also spoken in EU member states as a result of immigration. In many large EU cities it is said that hundreds of languages are spoken.

The presence of so many different languages inevitably means that a considerable number of staff are employed in translation work. This relates to both the written publication of documents and also the translation of speeches at EU meetings. With many meetings each day in the European Commission, European Parliament and Council of Ministers, the job of an interpreter is a high-pressure one where it is crucial to convey the importance of the points being made. This means that interpreters don't translate every word. Instead, they focus on the key points that a speaker is making. Sometimes it is particularly difficult to translate certain parts of a speech, such as jokes, where it is important that all of the delegates get the punchline at the same time.

One inevitable consequence of so much interpretation taking place is that from time to time suggestions emerge to reduce the number of languages. The vast majority of these suggestions are in fact spoofs designed to poke fun at the EU and so are not taken seriously.

Beyond the marketplace

Upon reflection it is evident that the SEA was a more profound agreement than many government leaders thought at the time. For a single market to be created there was a need for adjustments to be made to the role of the institutions to ensure the necessary free movement of people, goods, services and capital that lay at the heart of the single market programme. This required a strengthening in the supervisory powers of the European Commission to ensure that it was able to highlight non-compliance in any of the member states. To provide a democratic balance, the European Parliament was entrusted with new powers that meant that its co-operation was required when policies were being decided (the so-called co-operation procedure). A no less significant aspect was that the single market programme dramatically increased the workload of the European Court of Justice, which soon found itself faced with a whole raft of cases where companies and workers were not being allowed the access to markets that the legislation permitted.

The single market programme also influenced a desire and need to explore integration in other policy areas. The free movement of people created challenges arising from the impact of the migration of people across the EU. In time this would result in the need for greater EU integration in such areas as police and judicial co-operation to counter the removal of physical barriers between countries. On a day-to-day level other challenges arose from the fact that EU rules governing the single market meant that workers had to be treated in a similar manner across the EU. In the case of the medical community this meant that EU rules banned language tests for foreign doctors moving from one member state to another, thereby creating potentially complex situations where doctors have not always had a sufficient command of the national language where they are employed.

The increasing mobility of workers across the member states meant that a strong argument existed to develop some form of common working standards at the European level. Because people and companies were exchanging currencies on an ever more regular basis through trading relationships and visits to different countries, a number of commentators highlighted that the very process of currency exchange involved significant economic costs. Among a number of other reasons, there was a desire to look again at the practicalities for creating a single currency. These were issues that the new President of the European Commission, Jacques Delors, took to his heart when he stressed that the social objectives of the single market should have the same priority as its economic goals.

JACQUES DELORS

Born in Paris in 1925, Jacques Delors' early career at the Banque de France from 1945 to 1962 provided a solid foundation for a future career in the French government and European Commission. He served as Head of Social Affairs at the National Planning Board from 1962 to 1969 and as Chief Adviser on social affairs from 1969 to 1972. In 1974 he joined the French Socialist Party and would go on to take a number of senior roles, including serving as a Member of the European Parliament from 1979 to 1981, Minister for the Economy and Finance from 1981 to 1983 and then Minister for the Economy, Finance and Budget from 1983 to 1984. But it is in his role as the eighth President of the European Commission from 1985 to 1995 that he is best remembered. As President he played a pivotal role in the transformation of the Community into the European Union and served in office during a period of great change, including the creation of the single market programme, the collapse of the Berlin Wall, the break-up of the Soviet Union and the establishment of an agreement to create a single currency in the Maastricht Treaty. His strong leadership of the Commission inevitably created enemies within and outside his headquarters in Brussels. His desire to deepen European integration into policy areas that had traditionally rested with the member states often created a backlash from the more Eurosceptic member state governments. Britain's Prime Minister, Margaret Thatcher, was scathing of Delors's proposals to deepen European co-operation on social and monetary policy.

The Commission's desire to deepen European integration was also to be found on economic matters. In 1989 a report was published advocating the creation of a single currency. For some, the creation of a single currency represented a means of strengthening what were often regarded as weak currencies. But for Britain and others this represented an unacceptable move to the creation of a federal Europe and the downgrading of the influence of national governments. In the House of Commons on 30 October 1990 Prime Minister Thatcher famously said 'no, no, no' to Delors' proposals. This would be captured in the headline 'Up Yours Delors' that was published on 1 November 1990 in the British popular newspaper the *Sun*.

This brilliant and in many ways ludicrous piece of journalism conveyed a crucial and profound message about the Eurosceptic tide that was engulfing European politics. In essence, the headline marked a turning point when issues of European integration became central to the electoral strategy of political parties. Divisions within political parties and among the electorate marked the years that followed. Central to these concerns was the growing body of EU legislation – partly a response to the single market programme – that impacted on member states. Faced with such concerns, member state governments for the most part failed miserably to engage the public at the national level in a debate about European integration. And when they faced questions over the transfer of national decisions to the EU level their general response was to paper over concerns about the loss of sovereignty.

EUROSCEPTICISM

This term is generally used to refer to those who are opposed to European integration. The Eurosceptic camp is, however, a very broad one. On the one hand, it includes those individuals and groups who are opposed to membership of the EU. This comprises pressure groups and political parties that are prevalent in all member states, from the Danish People's Party to the German People's Union, and from the Austrian Freedom Party to the UK Independence Party. These political parties vary in their attitude to the EU. Some, such as the National Front in France and the UK

Independence Party are opposed to the concept of European integration and in extreme cases seek withdrawal. This is known as
'hard Euroscepticism'. On the other hand, there are those parties
who support membership of the EU, but who are opposed to specific EU policies and initiatives, such as a federal Europe, that take
too much power and influence away from the member state level.
Such a view is referred to as 'soft Euroscepticism'. Examples include
the Northern League in Italy and the Conservative Party in Britain.

Creating a European Union

The early 1990s saw the Community attempting to respond to a
fast-changing landscape caused by the fall of the Berlin Wall on
11 November 1989 and the subsequent break-up of the Soviet
controlled Communist governments in Central and Eastern
Europe in 1990. This would lead to the disintegration of the
Soviet Union in 1991. At the time, US President George H.W.
Bush referred to this as an event 'of almost biblical proportions'.

Such changes to the European landscape had been influenced
by a deliberate loosening of Soviet control on the countries of
Central and Eastern Europe since Mikhail Gorbachev's 1985
election as leader of the Soviet Union. Gorbachev was aware of
the need to restructure the Soviet economy and to create a more
open society at a time when the Soviet Union could not sustain
massive defence expenditure to maintain a balance of power with
the US. In the summer of 1989 Gorbachev announced that, in
response to growing unrest in Central and Eastern Europe, 'each
people determines the future of its own country. There must be
no interference from outside.' In these words Gorbachev ended
the Soviet policy of interference that had been enshrined in the
Brezhnev Doctrine. The implication of this was that Moscow no
longer had a legitimacy to intervene. This became known as the
Sinatra Doctrine, linking the decision to allow countries to go

their own way with the legendary American singer's most famous song, 'My Way'.

The upshot of these events was that a succession of Central and Eastern European countries undertook a process of reform with the ousting of their Communist regimes. Such changes were particularly stark in the case of Germany, which five decades after it had been divided once again became a unified country in October 1990. But while there was recognition of the necessity of German reunification, it was also true that a number of European leaders were alarmed at the prospect of an even stronger Germany being at the heart of Europe. Such concerns were particularly evident in the governments of France and Britain. Further afield, the US was concerned that the end of the Cold War would mean that the European Community would become overly focused on its own affairs and drift away from the transatlantic relationship.

The dramatic nature of the events that led to the reunification of Germany meant that there was pressure on the Community to respond to the challenges that lay ahead. Member state governments had already agreed that there was a need to look at the establishment of a single European currency after the publication of the April 1989 Delors Report. During the course of 1990 agreement was reached that the Community should also critically examine the working of its institutions and the scope of its broader policies in response to these events. This would result in the establishment of parallel intergovernmental conference (IGC) negotiations on political union and monetary union. These negotiations were intergovernmental because they comprised representatives of the member states and their purpose was to make amendments to the EC Treaties, just as the previous IGC discussions a few years earlier had resulted in the SEA.

The product of these talks was agreement in the Dutch town of Maastricht in December 1991 on a Treaty on European Union that deepened co-operation. A giant of a man in every way, the then German Chancellor, Helmut Kohl, would note that 'In Maastricht we laid the foundation-stone for the completion of the European Union. The European Union Treaty introduces a new and decisive stage in the process of European union, which within a few years will lead to the creation of what the founding fathers dreamed of after the last war: the United States of Europe.'

In truth, Kohl's view that a United States of Europe would emerge out of Maastricht was overly optimistic. Today the nation state continues to be King. However, Maastricht did make a number of crucial changes. A key feature of the Treaty was agreement being reached on establishing a single currency, to be known as the euro, by 1 January 1999. It would be another three years until, on 1 January 2002, euro banknotes and coins replaced national currencies.

At Maastricht member states also agreed to strengthen co-operation on social policy through the creation of a Social Chapter that extended the number of policy areas that were subject to majority voting, including the health and safety of workers, working conditions and sex equality. Agreement on social policy at Maastricht was, however, only possible after a deal was struck that excluded Britain from the Social Chapter. The British government of John Major had argued at Maastricht that EU intrusion into social policy reduced the competitiveness of British business. But the corollary of the Maastricht arrangement was to provide a clear imbalance to the objective of creating broad common standards that were in sympathy with the single market programme. This was deemed important to ensure that companies in one member state could not operate practices that were widely different from those of companies in other member states. This was particularly crucial because companies were increasingly operating on a pan-European basis that did not take account of national borders. Road haulage was a good example of this, whereby the transport of goods meant that French, Italian, Spanish and German drivers were as likely to be found on British roads as British drivers. Therefore it was important that such workers were governed by European and not national standards.

The Maastricht Treaty also changed the name of the Community to the European Union (EU), while new policies were added to the work of the EU.This included a stronger commitment to foreign and security policy and co-operation on interior affairs such as judicial policy, although the sensitive nature of their content meant that member state governments had been reluctant to give up control at the national level. Agreement was reached in a classic compromise that provided the scope for stronger co-operation at the European level and at the same time ensuring that each member state government retained influence through keeping the use of unanimity voting. This was achieved by creating policy silos that followed the design of a classical Roman temple. What this meant in practice was that co-operation on foreign and security policy as well as interior policy retained an intergovernmental structure that excluded other EU institutions such as the European Commission, European Parliament and Court of Justice. Instead, their influence was reserved solely for the first pillar that contained the bulk of the EU's common policies, from agriculture to the environment, and fisheries to the single market, and where qualified majority voting could be used.

The need to strengthen political co-operation, such as in the area of foreign and security policy and judicial co-operation, had been the result of necessity as the end of the Cold War eroded the gel that had kept the boundaries of many countries intact. In this sense, rather than being one state the Soviet Union was in essence a collection of states, of which some, such as the Baltic states of Latvia, Lithuania and Estonia, had been forcibly incorporated.The end of the Cold War removed some of the rationale for states to exist in their present configuration. In 1991 the Soviet Union fractured into fifteen states. Yugoslavia disintegrated during 1991 and 1992 and in1993 Czechoslovakia split into two countries.

Pillar structure of the European Union 1993–2009

Note: The Amsterdam Treaty provided for the responsibility for asylum, immigration and border controls to move to the first pillar. The pillar structure was abolished in the Lisbon Treaty, which came into effect on 1 December 2009.

Such changes meant that there was increasing pressure for the EU to deal with policies that required a European rather than a national response. But member states were cautious about transferring control to the EU over areas such as foreign and security policy. The outcome was an uncomfortable halfway house: the EU was nominally given responsibility for co-ordinating foreign and security policy without any real infrastructure back-up. This outcome paralysed the EU's ability to respond to crises such as the ethnic cleansing that took place in the former Yugoslavia during the 1990s.

Efforts to widen the EU's policy remit went hand-in-hand with initiatives to review the structure and working methods of the EU institutions. This included providing more powers to the European Parliament to ensure that there was a stronger democratic voice. Any attempt to quell concerns about the lack of democratic accountability in the EU had the opposite effect, as domestic parliamentarians, protest groups and the general public began to vent their hostility to what they considered to be the further erosion of national sovereignty. A consequence was that the governments of EU member states found the ratification of the Maastricht Treaty to be particularly problematic. A 'ratification crisis' emerged when the Danish electorate rejected the Treaty in a referendum vote on 2 June 1992. Having wanted to be the first to ratify the Treaty, the Danish 'no' vote triggered a wave of concern about the legitimacy of the new Treaty. Even though the Treaty was eventually passed in a second referendum in Denmark in May 1993 after the Danish government had secured concessions on defence policy and an opt out from the single currency, the process had created considerable uncertainty about the future path of European integration.

4

Creating a new Europe

Although all member states eventually ratified the Maastricht Treaty, the future of European integration had been seriously scarred. Concern about the EU's encroachment on domestic political affairs did not stem the enthusiasm of non-EU countries to seek membership. The number of applicant countries had been increased by the collapse of Communism in Central and Eastern Europe. A desire for membership was also to be found in Austria, Finland, Norway and Sweden. The governments of each of these countries took the same view that EU membership offered considerable economic benefits in terms of market access that offset any concerns about the impact on national sovereignty. The only potential exception was Norway, where there was a concern that membership would impact too much on traditional aspects of Norwegian life, such as fishing. But Norway was also in a more privileged position as North Sea oil receipts buoyed its economy. As a result the Norwegian electorate yet again rejected membership in a referendum vote in November 1994 in which 52% of the country's voters decided against membership. Thus, only Austria, Finland and Sweden joined the EU on 1 January 1995.

The 'Nordic' enlargement brought the EU's membership to fifteen. The infrastructure, institutions and methods of decision making in the EU were for the most part able to cope with what was essentially an unproblematic enlargement. The countries were economically and politically developed and placed few financial demands on the EU. By contrast, the potential for the EU to enlarge to include five, ten or maybe more states from Central and Eastern Europe necessitated a more detailed analysis of how the EU worked than was provided in the Maastricht Treaty.

After nearly forty years of existence, the EU had consistently ducked the question as to why its budget continued to be dominated by agricultural policy. This was a particularly important issue because the majority of the prospective members had large agricultural sectors. As a consequence the EU would have to offer financial support that exceeded what it was able to give. The untenable nature of this situation combined with the need to consider basic but nonetheless important questions – such as whether every member state should have a European Commissioner, meant that there was a need for further Treaty reform.

WHO CAN JOIN THE EU?

Although in theory any European country can apply to join the EU, membership is based on a specific set of criteria that were agreed to at the June 1993 Copenhagen European Council, otherwise known as the Copenhagen criteria. This states that countries must have:

1. Stable institutions that guarantee democracy, the rule of law, human rights and respect for and protection of minorities;
2. A functioning market economy and the capacity to cope with competitive pressure and market forces within the EU;
3. The ability to take on the obligations of membership, including adherence to the aims of political and Economic and Monetary Union (EMU).

When a country makes an application for membership the Commission provides an initial assessment. If the initial view is positive then the applicant state in conjunction with the Commission starts a process of establishing aspects of national legislation that will have to be altered as well as highlighting potential hurdles to membership, such as where there might be a difficulty in adapting its legislation. The EU often provides various forms of economic, political and legal support that helps the applicant state to meet the requirements of membership. Thereafter formal negotiations begin between the applicant state and the Commission, which can result in an agreement that grants a period of transition with regard to membership. This therefore allows the applicant to delay implementing certain aspects of EU legislation for a specified period after they become a member state. Finally, once the negotiations have been conducted, the Council of Ministers and the European Parliament both have to give their approval for the applicant state to join. Sometimes the applicant state also holds a referendum on membership, whereby it allows its electorate to decide whether they would like to join. This can result in a rejection in the terms of membership, as in the case of Norway.

Enlargement also necessitates the EU to change. This can include adjustments to the institutions, such as the number of votes each member state gets in the Council of Ministers. There might also have to be changes to the EU budget to take account of the costs of enlargement.

Bigger, but not better

While the Maastricht Treaty was supposed to provide the EU with the structures and policies that would enable it to operate in an effective manner and deal with the challenges it faced, it quickly became apparent that there were flaws in its design. New policies, such as foreign and security policy, were hindered by rather rudimentary working methods. The EU had the potential to send troops into conflict zones to secure peace, but there were virtually no military personnel in the EU's headquarters in Brussels. Control continued to rest with member state governments. The problem with this was that the governments could not agree on what to do. When the former Yugoslavia broke up in the early 1990s, member states were unable and unwilling to reach a consensus on how to stop the bitter ethnic conflict that emerged. This mainly took place between Serbs and the Croats and Bosniaks. The conflicts were the deadliest in Europe since 1945 and were the first since the end of the Second World War to be judged as genocide, with the key perpetrators being charged with war crimes and often being brought before the International Criminal Tribunal for the former Yugoslavia that was established by the United Nations.

The fragility of the EU's collective security and defence policy was highlighted a few years later when the American-backed NATO rather than the EU was tasked with ending the humanitarian crisis that unfolded in Kosovo. In 1999 NATO, the most powerful military alliance the world has ever seen, commenced a process of bombing the small state of Serbia to get it to withdraw its paramilitary forces from Kosovo where they were engaged in a systematic process of murdering and displacing the majority ethnic Albanian population. This action alone lasted seventy-nine days until the Serbian forces withdrew.

Some of the lessons from issues such as these were tackled in the Treaty of Amsterdam, which was agreed to at the Amsterdam European Council of June 1997. The Amsterdam Treaty, which became law in 1999, set out a number of significant changes, most notably the decision to create a new position to co-ordinate foreign and security policy. The appointee would be called the High Representative. Other changes included the creation of an area of freedom, security and justice to ensure that the free movement of persons was matched with protection for citizens through co-operation between police and judicial authorities in member states. For example, the breakdown in barriers between countries had created a haven for organised criminal activity and the EU needed to strengthen its response to these challenges.

From the late 1990s there was a growing concern that EU policies needed to focus on dealing with the high levels of employment in many member states. This would lead to agreement in March 2000 on a 'Lisbon Strategy' for growth and jobs. The aim was simple: to make the EU the most competitive economy in the world and to achieve full employment by 2010. Such a focus took account of the economic competition that the EU faced from developing economies such as China and India. The strategy set a number of specific targets, such as an average annual economic growth rate of 3% and an overall employment participation rate of 70%. But while there were clear merits to such a strategy, the decade that followed was dominated by regular reports noting that the Lisbon Strategy was heading for failure. In the end, the strategy did not deliver the objectives that had been expected. To a large extent this was not surprising given the economic difficulties that beset many EU countries at this time, particularly spiralling levels of public debt, low economic growth, a reduction in the GDP of member states and relatively high unemployment.

The European Commission's own analysis of the Lisbon Strategy notes that while the strategy has had some notable benefits, such as economic growth being linked to a downward use of energy, the 'catch-all' nature of the guidelines that accompanied the strategy meant that they were not sufficiently tailored to the individual demands of member states. This reflects the difficulty of establishing common EU policies and objectives across twenty-seven member states with different economies and structures of governance. The problem that the EU faces is therefore one of trying to create strategies that foster greater economic growth and increase cohesiveness, coupled with the fact that the economic gulf separating the richest and poorest member states will always impact on the ability to deliver such a strategy.

Yet, despite these concerns, the EU is also wedded at the hip to producing such strategies. Thus, in 2010 the Commission published 'Europe 2020: A European Strategy for smart, sustainable and inclusive growth'. Its aim is to guide the EU out of economic recession and to raise employment, productivity and social cohesion.

A constitutional conundrum

Although the adjustments made by the likes of the Amsterdam and Lisbon Treaties were designed to improve the way some policies operated, they did not really get to the heart of preparing the EU for enlargement so as to accommodate the large number of countries that wished to join. The EU's automatic response to this situation was for the member states to meet again with a view to agreeing yet another Treaty. The conclusion of these discussions was the Treaty of Nice, which was agreed to in December 2000 and became law on 1 February 2003. Just as with previous Treaties, the final outcome was a mixed compromise. Limits were placed on each member state having one European Commissioner each, thereby ending the right of Britain, France, Italy, Germany and Spain to have two Commissioners. The number of Members of the European Parliament was also adjusted to provide room for the applicant countries.

In 2004, one year after the Treaty of Nice became law, the EU undertook the biggest enlargement in its history, with the accession of ten member states: Cyprus, Czech Republic, Estonia, Hungary, Latvia, Lithuania, Malta, Poland, Slovakia and Slovenia. As a result, the EU's membership increased from fifteen to twenty-five, while some hundred million people were added to its population.

More than anything else, this enlargement fundamentally changed the make-up and future direction of the EU. In short, it once and for all emphasised that the EU needed to undertake a root and branch reform of its working methods rather than adopting a more piecemeal approach of incremental change, as had been the case with previous Treaty reforms. A desire for change was for the most part to be found in the member states as well as the EU institutions themselves. Evidence of the need for a more considered review included the fact that a number of archaic and potentially anarchic decision-making procedures had evolved. For instance, the European Commission was responsible for the EU external relations, including such activities as humanitarian aid and overseas diplomatic representation. At the same time, however, it was the Council of Ministers that was responsible for the EU's foreign and security policy. Both policies clearly impacted on the other and yet they were not part of an integrated single strategy.

These issues were wrapped into a series of debates that took place at the Convention on the Future of Europe, which was chaired by the former French President Valery Giscard d'Estaing and met between March 2002 and June 2003. The Convention was a rather grand body that included a range of representatives from the EU institutions, member state governments and national parliaments. The member states were clearly not in control of the process, including the recommendations that emerged from the discussions, which took the form of a draft Constitutional Treaty in June 2003. A number of governments were particularly concerned by the term 'Constitutional Treaty' as the very creation of an EU Constitution raised significant issues about the transfer of sovereignty away from the member states.

The draft Constitutional Treaty provided the basis for yet another IGC negotiation that commenced in October 2003 and finished at the Brussels European Council of June 2004 where agreement was reached on a new EU Constitutional Treaty. At face value, there was some sense in this outcome as it tidied up what was in essence a rather haphazard set of rules that governed the EU. Somewhat predictably the Treaty proposed the extension of majority voting in the Council of Ministers to even more policy areas because the expansion of EU membership to what were now twenty-five member states made it impossible to secure agreement on a unanimous basis. Notable changes included the creation of a new post of EU President, which would dispense with the existing system of each member state taking it in turns on a six-monthly basis to organise the workings of the Council of Ministers and the European Council. Yet again, as membership expanded, the rationale for the rotating system had become harder to justify. This was not just because it took longer for each member state to take on the presidency role of the Presidency (every twelve and half years in an EU of twenty-five member states), but also because some were better able than others to take on this task. A final notable area of change included the creation of a new EU Minister for Foreign Affairs that would combine the existing positions of the Council's High Representative for foreign policy and the European Commissioner for external relations.

What happened next has become a salient lesson for governments and EU institutions that had essentially lost contact with the electorate. The majority of the public could not see the rationale for the transfer of more power away from the member states to the EU. Member state governments had regularly failed to explain to their electorate the true significance of European integration. Governments would return from EU meetings and proclaim that a decision had been achieved that defended the national interest. But no agreement could ever reflect all the interests of each member state. Compromise was essential and this meant that there would inevitably be winners and losers in every negotiation. Yet it was rare for a government to explain to their electorate that the interconnected nature of the EU meant that decisions would often be taken that served the majority EU viewpoint rather than the individual national interest. The end result was that the Treaty ran into the buffers in the summer of

2005 when it was rejected in referendums in France and the Netherlands. EU leaders did not say it at the time, but the Constitutional Treaty was dead.

There still remained the issue of tackling practical issues surrounding the way that the EU institutions worked and the manner by which decisions were taken. After a short hiatus, the Treaty bandwagon resurrected itself in June 2007 when agreement was reached that negotiations should commence again on what would be termed a 'Reform Treaty'. Such discussions would now include Bulgaria and Romania as they joined the EU on 1 January 2007. The upshot of these developments was member states agreeing to a revised Treaty at the December 2007 Lisbon European Council. And because of the practice of naming these Treaties after the city in which they were finally negotiated, it became known as the Lisbon Treaty. After a period of discussion in the member states, the Treaty finally entered into law on 1 December 2009.

A notable significance of the Lisbon Treaty was that it abolished the three-pillar structure that had been established by the Maastricht Treaty nearly two decades before. The intervening period had witnessed a gradual strengthening of co-operation on foreign policy and interior affairs to the extent that it was no longer evident that these policy areas could be deemed as purely the responsibility of the member states. Indeed if anything the reality was that there was a need for a stronger and more effective method of co-operation on what had become important policy areas that dealt with critical issues, from dealing with so-called failed states such as Somalia to combating terrorism and human trafficking.

The end of the Treaty road?

IGC negotiations have been a regular feature of European integration throughout the last twenty years and have emphasised the extent to which the EU decision-making process has reflected intergovernmental rather than supranational design. Because all member states have to be in agreement with the final Treaty for it to become a reality, individual leaders inevitably have to compromise on many of their initial negotiating positions. The various IGC negotiations have made a number of significant changes to the EU, including altering the decision-making structure and extending its remit into new policy areas. Such changes have been prompted by a number of factors, including the desire to make the EU more competitive with regard to such advanced industrial economies as the United States and Japan, as well as the emerging economic powerhouses of Brazil, India, Russia and China (the so-called BRIC group of countries). But at the same time, the expansion of EU membership from six to twenty-seven member states over the last seven decades has been a further important factor influencing change.

EU Treaty Reform

Treaty	Signed	Took effect	Key Developments
Treaty of Paris	1951	1952	European Coal and Steel Community (ECSC)
Treaties of Rome	1957	1958	European Atomic Energy Community (Euratom) and European Economic Community (EEC)
Treaty Establishing a Single Council and a Single Commission of the European Communities	1965	1967	Merger of the executives of the three different institutions (ECSC, Euratom, EEC)
Single European Act	1986	1987	Single Market

Cont'd

Treaty	Signed	Took effect	Key Developments
Treaty on European Union (Maastricht Treaty)	1992	1993	Economic and Monetary Union (EMU) and Common Foreign and Security Policy (CFSP)
Treaty of Amsterdam	1997	1999	Institutional reform, including post of High Representative for foreign and security policy
Treaty of Nice	2001	2003	Institutional reform
Treaty of Lisbon	2007	2009	Institutional reform, including creation of permanent Council President

Although the excitement and concern caused by the failure of the Constitutional Treaty and its subsequent replacement by the Lisbon Treaty was most keenly registered among a small group of political leaders, the outcome of such negotiations had a considerable impact on the wider European electorate. While the Treaty produced an outcome that included the usual sort of compromises that offset deeper integration in one policy and the retaining of national vetoes in others, the prolonged nature of the negotiations potentially signals the end of the road for such big set-piece intergovernmental conference negotiations.

A key reason behind this analysis is the financial crisis that has gripped the international economy since 2008, having a particularly noticeable impact on the EU, especially the eurozone countries. In the face of a financial storm that has seen rioting in EU member states in response to the imposition of austerity measures, such as budget and wage cuts, there has emerged a question mark over the desirability of further European integration given increasing domestic discontent about the EU. To this end there is a body of opinion that the EU's policies often do not reflect the challenges of individual member states, which are often to do with core issues such as welfare and employment and for which the blanket nature of EU policies does not always provide the correct answer. A key challenge for the EU is accordingly the need to clarify the goals and limits of European integration in the context of a diverse composition of member states. This in itself will not be an easy process and will potentially result in accepted divisions between those member states who wish to progress integration into wider and deeper areas of policy and those who wish to retract to an EU that is principally driven by the need to foster economic competitiveness and maximise trading opportunities.

5

The muscles from Brussels: the European Commission

The European Commission is the best-known of all the EU institutions. Its recognition stems from the fact that in most areas of EU policy it has the responsibility for initiating new legislation. At the same time it has the task of running the EU on a day-to-day basis, from managing routine policies such as agriculture through to organising the EU's response to humanitarian disasters. What this means in practice is that the European Commission combines both the executive functions of policy initiation that are to be found in national governments with the administrative functions of a civil service.

At the pinnacle of the European Commission is its President, who leads a team of European Commissioners who represent each of the member states and are appointed for a five-year term of office. For all intents and purposes Commissioners are the equivalent of national government ministers. The President is the most powerful official in the EU and is responsible for the Commission's strategic leadership, in a similar vein to the Prime Minister or President of a national government. As such, the Commission is often referred to by the surname of the President in office, from its first President Walter Hallstein who held office from 1958 to 1967 (Hallstein Commission) to

José Manuel Barroso's two periods in office from 2004 to 2014 (Barroso Commission). In undertaking their duties, the European Commissioners are supported by tiers of officials who deal with specific policies such as the environment, education and rural development.

Analysis of the European Commission tends to fall into two camps. The first is that the Commission is the gravitational centre of the European integration process that is eroding national sovereignty. Such an argument depicts the Commission as being the 'belly of the beast' of the European project. A contrasting view is that the Commission fulfils a key role at the heart of Europe, by administering everyday policies that affect European citizens and also playing an important part in establishing common policies. And while both camps see the Commission at the centre of Europe, the first views it as an unnecessary institution. Yet the reality is that while the Commission can rightly be subject to criticism, and even though the member states do not have an equivalent type of institution, the Commission has from the outset played an important role in running the EU.

The Commission plays an important role because it has traditionally been responsible for initiating new legislation that influences daily lives, such as clean water and hours at work. Such legislation is specifically known as regulations, decisions and directives. Of these three forms of legislation, regulations are directly applicable on the member states concerned. In other words a member state does not have to set out specific measures at a national level to implement the European policy. Examples of regulations – which can be passed by either the European Commission acting alone or by the EU Council of Ministers and the European Parliament – include the 2004 Commission Regulation (261/2004), which established common rules on compensation and assistance to passengers in the event of them being denied the boarding of an aircraft, or of the cancellation or long delays to their flight. In 2010 EU Council Regulation

(961/2010) was implemented to impose restrictive measures to hinder Iran developing a nuclear programme. As a result, this regulation prohibits European companies from making new investments in the Iranian oil and gas sector, as well as prohibiting the export of key goods. Other examples of regulations include the 2006 Council Regulation (510/2006) on the protection of products from geographical areas, such as Parma ham.

In contrast to the unbinding nature of regulations, directives set out aims that member states need to adhere to, but crucially the member states are given the flexibility to determine the methods and approach with regard to achieving these aims. For example, although the 1993 European Council Directive on Working Time (93/104/EC) set specific working conditions, including a maximum forty-eight-hour week, member state governments implemented the legislation in different ways, including the ability of workers to opt out of the maximum working week.

Finally, decisions are directly binding upon the member states or individuals to which they are addressed. For example, in 2003 EU decisions (189, 190 and 191) introduced the European Health Insurance Card into national security systems. This allows EU citizens who are temporarily staying in the territory of the European Economic Area (which comprises the twenty-seven EU member states plus Iceland, Liechtenstein and Norway) or Switzerland, such as when on holiday or on business, to access state-provided healthcare at either reduced cost or free of charge.

Beyond a policy initiation function, the Commission's roles have varied from administering key policies such as agriculture, employment and social policy, the environment, regional policy and trade, to being the guardian of the Treaties and the *acquis communitaire* (i.e. all the Community's legislation). The Commission also monitors compliance, so that if member states and companies do not adhere to legislation then it can refer legal proceedings to the Court of Justice. It also undertakes a mediation role between member states and institutions in order to reach a compromise and acts as the EU's diplomatic representative to non-EU countries and a multitude of international organisations.

As a consequence the Commission has had a significant role in shaping the evolution of the EU and when new EU policies emerge they tend to be presented as if the 'Commission has decided'. This is not a coincidence. This is because the founding fathers of European integration deliberately designed a strong Commission that would be capable of pulling together the interests of different member states to form a strong and coherent organisation. The implication of this was that the years that followed were marked by a number of strategies to provide a more balanced institutional structure.

Belly of the beast or the heart of Europe?

Much of the day-to-day work of administering EU policies is undertaken by the Commission, which employs a staff of approximately thirty-four thousand people, who are often referred to in the media as 'Eurocrats'. Multinational in nature, staff are appointed by means of competitive examination to serve the European interest over their own national interests. Member states are aware of the fact that it is very helpful if their own citizens gain positions in the Commission as well as in the other EU institutions. The reason for this is quite obvious: such individuals are more likely to be aware of and potentially sympathetic to the causes that are championed by the member state. It is additionally easier for a member state to be able to influence the EU institutions when there are officials who speak the same language and share the same cultural background. But despite the benefits to a member state of its nationals working in the EU institutions, not all member states have been as swift footed in advancing this cause. Even though Britain established a 'European Fast stream' in 1990 to prepare officials for future employment in the EU institutions, by 2010 British citizens only accounted for 1.8% of staff at entry level grades in the European Commission despite the fact that Britain accounts for approximately 12% of the EU population.

The number of staff it employs influences the way the Commission performs its tasks. On the one hand the Commission can be viewed as excessively bureaucratic. Yet on the other, the Commission is relatively small in terms of its staffing. It is comparable to a medium-sized city council in Britain. The outcome of this state of affairs, namely the relatively small size of its staff and the range of policies that fall within its remit, means that the Commission is often unfairly criticised for poor performance. Such criticism requires further clarification because given the small number of Commission staff, the responsibility for implementing and administering policies often rests with the member states that tend to be resistant to its efforts. This can lead to foot dragging and non-compliance at the national level. A particular area where the Commission has been subject to criticism is in the realm of expenditure programmes, where the size and complexity of the budget have made it vulnerable to waste and mismanagement. In 2010 for the sixteenth year running, the European Court of Auditors refused to sign off the EU's accounts, noting that 'payments from the budget continue to be materially affected by error'.

Just as is the case with national governments, the policies that fall within the Commission's remit are divided into a variety of organisational units. As the table below indicates, the majority of these are known as Directorates General (DG) and the remaining are referred to as specialised services. Inevitably there is a considerable distinction between the importance and size of the DGs and specialised services. As agriculture accounts for around 40%

of EU budgetary expenditure it should not be surprising that DG agriculture employs approximately one thousand staff, while at the other extreme DG Education and Culture employs around 150 staff. A direct result of this is that some DGs are seen to be more important than others and large member states are keen to ensure that 'their' Commissioner is responsible for key areas of the Commission's work. In terms of structure, each of the DGs is headed by a Director General, who is the senior official responsible for the policies within the specific DG and is normally a career official appointed by the European Commission. The Director General in turn reports to an individual European Commissioner responsible for that area of work. This is similar to, say, a senior civil servant heading a government department, with a government minister – or in this sense the European Commissioner – having the political responsibility for the policy. And just as government ministers are supported by a close knit group of advisers, so too are Commissioners, who are supported by a group of officials known as a Cabinet who are chosen by the individual Commissioner. Their purpose is to provide advice on policy initiatives, of which large proportions are citizens of the European Commissioner's own nation. Heads of Cabinet meet every week with the primary purpose of clearing issues prior to, or after, meetings of the European Commission.

EUROPEAN COMMISSION DIRECTORATES GENERAL, 2012

Agriculture and Rural Development (AGRI)
Budget (BUDG)
Climate Action (CLIMA)
Communication (COMM)
Economic and Financial Affairs (ECFIN)
Education and Culture (EAC)

Employment, Social Affairs and Inclusion (EMPL)
Energy (ENER)
Enlargement (ELARG)
Enterprise and Industry (ENTR)
Environment (ENV)
EuropeAid Development and Co-operation (DEVCO)
Eurostat (ESTAT)
Foreign Policy Instruments Service (EEAS)
Health and Consumers (SANCO)
Home Affairs (Home)
Humanitarian Aid (ECHO)
Human Resources and Security (HR)
Informatics (DIGIT)
Information Society and Media (INFSO)
Internal Market and Services (MARKT)
Interpretation (SCIC)
Joint Research Centre (JRC)
Justice (JUST)
Maritime Affairs and Fisheries (MARE)
Mobility and Transport (MOVE)
Regional Policy (REGIO)
Research and Innovation (RTD)
Secretariat General (SG)
Taxation and Customs Union (TAXUD)
Trade (TRADE)
Translation (DGT)

European Commissioners

In every sense it is the twenty-seven European Commissioners who are the driving force of the Commission. At the moment there is one European Commissioner from each member state, who is appointed for a five-year (renewable) term of office having been recommended by national governments. Up until 2005 there were two Commissioners from each of the larger member states (Britain, Germany, France, Italy and Spain) and one from the smaller states. Enlargement to Central and Eastern Europe necessitated a rethinking of this practice to ensure that the Commission did not continue to expand exponentially. Even now with twenty-seven Commissioners there is a concern that there are too many. But the prospect of a member state not having a Commissioner filled some heads of state and government with horror, and so agreement was reached in 2008 that every member state will have a Commissioner.

Although Commissioners are not, or should not, be open to influence or direct orders from their national governments as they represent the European ideals of the European project, it is inevitably the case that each Commissioner cannot just detach themselves from their ties with their own member state. Some would argue that one strength of the Commission is the fact that it contains a representative from each member state, and of course the member states would have been conscious of the need for 'their' Commissioner to best represent their interests when nominating a Commissioner for appointment. Commissioners have tended to be politicians who have occupied senior office in their respective member state, although some Commissioners have been businessmen, trade union leaders and senior administrators. As European Commissioners are nominated by national governments, they are in every sense 'unelected' even though their appointment is subject to the approval of the European Parliament. This is not to say that the Commission is unaccountable. The Commission cannot operate in a political vacuum and the Council of Ministers and the European Parliament fill that vacuum.

THE APPOINTMENT OF EUROPEAN COMMISSIONERS

The appointment process for a European Commissioner begins at a national level, with a member state government nominating a suitable candidate in consultation with the Commission President.

Once agreement has been reached, the Commissioner is then sub-
jected to hearings at the European Parliament, which votes on
their suitability.

Critics of European Commissioners inevitably point to the
undemocratic nature of the appointment process. For example, it is
noticeable that Commissioners have tended to be male, with
women being under-represented, while no ethnic minorities have
to date been appointed a European Commissioner. Criticism is
often levied at the way that member state governments use their
power to appoint Commissioners as a means of rewarding or pla-
cating national politicians. There has also been concern that
Commissioners – who are not supposed to represent national
interests – have become increasingly politicised by intervening
in national affairs. In 2007 the Belgian Commissioner, Louis
Michel, took leave to stand in the Belgian parliamentary elections.
Such a stance is indicative of the tendency of Commissioners
to leave to take up a position in their member state government.
Lord Peter Mandelson resigned from the Commission in 2008
to return to British politics as a member of Gordon Brown's
government.

Commission President

The political effectiveness of the Commission depends upon the
influence of the President of the European Commission, who is
responsible for leading and directing the organisation. The
appointment of the President is subject to a great deal of lobbying and influence by the member state governments. Such is the
significance of the President that Commission Presidencies are
often referred to by the name of the incumbent President, which
for better or worse conjures up an instant image of the 'success'
of the work programme conducted by all the Commissioners.

The extent to which one Commission is deemed to be more successful than another is influenced by a whole of range of factors, including luck. The global and national environment of member states is particularly important. The first Commission President, Walter Hallstein, was a dominant figure with the task of bringing the different interests of the member states together into a cohesive organisation. The mid-1960s witnessed a revolt against the integration that inevitably arose out of Hallstein's efforts, with the French President Charles de Gaulle seeking to repatriate influence back to the national level. This meant that the pendulum of influence swung away from the Commission to the member states in the form of the workings of the Council of Ministers and the European Council and this would continue until the mid-1980s.

The deepening of European integration that took place over a decade from the mid-1980s to the mid-1990s was greatly attributed to Commission President Jacques Delors. But while the Delors Presidency was an extremely active one and heralded agreement on triumphant policies such as the single market and single currency, his legacy is nevertheless contested. Some individuals argue that there would have been little or no development of the EU's policies without his leadership. Others argue that he benefited from a more buoyant global economy as well as the willingness of member state governments to address some of the problems that had arisen. But irrespective of these viewpoints, it is evident that since Delors left office the Commission has not had a President who has matched his leadership, energy and vision. And while José Manuel Barroso, who has been President of the Commission since 2004, has sought to offer leadership, his period in office has been battered by the difficulties over the failed Constitutional Treaty, international economic problems and the eurozone financial crisis.

Presidents of the European Commission

1958–67	Walter Hallstein (West Germany)	Central to establishing the role of the Commission as the engine of European integration.
1967–70	Jean Rey (Belgium)	A cautious leader who failed to reassert the Commission's role after the 1965 empty chair crisis.
1970–2	Franco Malfatti (Italy)	A weak leader who presided over an undistinguished period in office that would eventually result in him resigning.
1972–3	Sicco Mansholt (Netherlands)	An interim President after the resignation of Malfatti.
1973–7	François-Xavier Ortoli (Italy)	Largely an ineffective President. His role was not helped by the economic difficulties that were caused by the 1973–4 oil crisis.
1977–81	Roy Jenkins (UK)	Attempted to reassert the Commission's leadership role, evidenced by his efforts to develop the European Monetary System (EMS) and establishing the right of the Commission President to attend world economic summits.
1981–5	Gaston Thorn (Luxembourg)	An undistinguished tenure that provided little in the way of substantive achievements.
1985–94	Jacques Delors (France)	Played a major role in leading the EU through a period of considerable transformation, highlighted by the completion of the single market, agreement on monetary union and establishing the foundations for enlargement.

Cont'd

1995–99	Jacques Santer (Luxembourg)	Although he realised notable achievements such as enlargement, monetary union and the development of a common foreign and security policy, he was regarded as a complacent leader.
1999–2004	Romano Prodi (Italy)	While his period in office witnessed the birth of the single currency, agreements on enlargement to Central and Eastern Europe and efforts to reform the EU, he is regarded as a disorganised President.
2004–14	José Manuel Barroso (Portugal)	His period in office has seen some of the greatest challenges to the EU, notably the response to the war on terror, enlargement, institutional reform and the financial crisis.

Commission as agenda setter

What is unique about the Commission is that its role extends beyond being the administrative hub responsible for managing a multitude of EU policies. Its role also includes having sole responsibility for initiating legislation within the EU, thereby ensuring that its remit is significantly different from that of a national civil service. A consequence of this dual implementation and administration role is that it is impossible to compare the Commission with any other body or organisation in the world. This uniqueness means that people inevitably have different views about the sort of function the Commission should play. For some, its ability to initiate legislation means that it should be viewed as an autonomous actor capable of making independent decisions and championing policies that are in the European interest. For others, it is merely an agent of the member states, existing to initiate and administer the sort of policies favoured by national governments.

As the Commission has a monopoly on initiating legislation, EU law cannot be made without its proposals. All of this has meant that the Commission has become a target for the lobbying efforts of national governments, business interests, trade unions, as well as other EU institutions such as the European Parliament. This includes member state governments who have Permanent Representations to the EU that are based in Brussels and which are totally separate from the national Embassy to Belgium that is also based in Brussels. The Permanent Representations act as a forward staging post that seeks to influence the national view-point in the EU institutions and other member state representa-tions, as well as to act as a listening post that informs the formulation of policy back home. Most member states are not content with just this national representation, and instead you will find on a visit to Brussels a plethora of representative offices from local and regional government. Such a development has been influenced by the growth of EU regional policy (thereby attracting regions seeking financial support from the EU) and the trend towards devolution in many member states. In Britain there are representative offices from the Scottish Executive, the Welsh Assembly Government and the Northern Ireland Executive, as well as from regional government such as the office of the West Midlands in Europe.

THE COMMISSION'S ROLE IN INITIATING EU LEGISLATION

Although the genesis of the ideas that result in EU legislation can come from a variety of sources, such as member state governments, lobby groups and the EU institutions themselves, the formal process begins with a law being drafted in the relevant Directorate General of the Commission and then concludes with implementation in the member states. As a result, the progress of legislation tends to follow a similar route:

Legislative proposals are drafted in the appropriate Directorate General.

⇓

Proposals are then reviewed by the Commission Legal Service and other relevant Directorate Generals.

⇓

European Commissioners review the proposals.

⇓

If agreement is reached among the Commissioners, proposals are sent to the Council of Ministers and the European Parliament for their decision.

⇓

Finally proposals are implemented in member states.

You will also find a gamut of countries and organisations seeking to influence policy outcomes at the EU level. This can range from large countries such as China and the US to micro-states such as the Seychelles. There are in addition representatives from multinational corporations, charities, industry, trade unions and special interest groups. As part of an effort to allay public concern over the potential for interest representatives to gain excessive influence in the EU, the Commission established a code of conduct for interest representation and compiled a register of representation. As of January 2011 there were 3,308 interest representatives in the register ranging from the Church of Sweden to the largest company in the world, General Electric.

LOBBYING AND THE TOBACCO
ADVERTISING DIRECTIVE

A good example of lobbying at the EU level concerns the Tobacco Advertising Directive of 30 July 1998, which banned all commercial communication (such as direct-mailing and night-club promotions) or sponsorship that aimed to promote tobacco products. This Directive was particularly significant as it had a direct impact on a number of interested parties: the tobacco industry, the advertising industry, the Formula One motor industry, as well as member states who were themselves divided on the question. The Directive was subject to a considerable amount of lobbying at both the level of the EU institutions and member states (notably Britain) by tobacco firms and the Formula One racing industry, all of which were concerned over the potential loss of revenue. The very nature of the EU policy process meant that pressure groups had multiple channels in which they could seek to exercise influence.

On 1 October 1997 Max Mosley, the President of the Féderation Internationale de l'Automobile (FIA), the governing body for world motor sport, wrote to the British Health Minister, Tessa Jowell, to argue for an exemption from the Directive for the Formula One racing industry on the basis that the sport would leave Europe for other countries that did not have as stringent regulations, and that jobs would be lost. To sweeten the pill, Mosley offered voluntary worldwide restrictions on advertising that included the removal of logos from the helmets of the racing drivers. On 4 November 1997 the British Labour government argued that there should be a full exemption for the Directive for the tobacco sponsorship of Formula One, with some commentators accusing Prime Minister Tony Blair of sleaze when it emerged that the Labour Party had received a £1 million donation from Grand Prix boss Bernie Ecclestone before the 1997 general election.

In the end, member states agreed to implement the Directive, with a deadline of 31 July 2005 being set to comply with its provisions. For Formula One, this meant that cigarette brand names had to be removed from their cars. Concern over the loss of lucra-tive sponsorship from the tobacco industry has, however, meant that many of the cars continue to bear the colours and designs associated with the brands that provide the financial backing.

In undertaking a policy initiation role, the Commission attempts to reflect what is best for the EU as a whole. There is no set pattern for the way that a particular initiative materialises. Initiatives can emerge as a result of the suggestions of a member state or a lobby group from the judgements of the Court of Justice, from requests by the European Parliament or the Council of Ministers, from considering legislation that is already in place, as well as from reports or research that the Commission has spon-sored. Notable examples of the latter include the 1985 White Paper on completing the single market and the 1989 Delors Report on monetary union. And while individual European Commissioners are crucial to this process by providing political leadership to direct policy initiatives, Commissioners do more than just implement and administer laws and procedures. They see themselves as the guardians of the spirit of the EU. And as the Treaties have referred to such things as 'ever closer union' it is not surprising that the Commission is associated with proposing deeper integration and has been called the 'motor of European integration', given its role in initiating new policies and its responsibility for administering existing policies.

Roles and responsibilities

The staff employed by the Commission perform an important administrative role by managing the sort of policy areas that are commonly found in most national governments. Today the

Commission's responsibilities extend from education to employment and from transport to trade. Within these policies the Commission's influence can vary. On matters of education policy, the Commission's role is primarily concerned with championing pan-EU interests. This includes ensuring that national qualifications in each member state are accepted on a European basis. The Commission is also active in supporting research and collaboration on a Europe-wide basis. This contrasts with trade policy where the member states have delegated to the Commission responsibility for conducting trade negotiations with individual countries as well as through multilateral trade rounds that take place in the form of the World Trade Organisation (WTO). Over 100 countries have agreements with the EU. And while preferential trade agreements also exist for the former colonies of the member states to assist with their economic development, other countries can regard such agreements as anti-competitive. There is a practical reason for the Commission to have responsibility on trade matters: the combined influence of the EU-twenty-seven is going to be greater when negotiating with the likes of China, Russia or America than if Britain or Germany were to negotiate on an individual basis.

A crucial task performed by the Commission is managing the EU's annual budget, which in 2011 totalled €141.9 billion. Although a large sum, the budget is smaller than the budget of a medium EU member state such as Austria or Belgium. Moreover, when put in a broader comparative perspective, the size of the EU budget is dwarfed by the total government spending of the twenty-seven EU member states, which is nearly fifty times that of the EU budget. Nonetheless, the EU budget has been subject to considerable debate, with critics pointing out that its balance towards agriculture does not reflect the overall decline in the significance of agriculture to the European economy. Some member states, such as France, have been unwilling to reduce the amount of money given to their farmers. Indeed, it is noticeable that in 2009 France received the largest share of EU budget expenditure, which amounted to €13.6 billion. However, when calculated on the basis of percentage of Gross National Income, Lithuania received the greatest amount at 6.73%.

EU Budget 2012

Spending area	(€ billion)	% of total budget
Sustainable growth	67.5	48.11
1a Competitiveness for growth and employment	14.7	10.0
1b Cohesion for growth and employment	52.7	35.8
2 Preservation and management of natural resources	60.0	40.8
2a *of which Direct aids & market related expenditure*	44.0	29.9
2b *of which Rural development, environment & fisheries*	15.9	10.8
3 Citizenship, freedom, security and justice	2.1	1.4
3a Freedom, security and justice	1.4	0.9
3b Citizenship	0.7	0.5
4 EU as a global player	9.4	6.4
5 Administration	8.3	5.6
of which for the Commission	3.3	2.3
Total	147.2	100
In % of EU Gross National Income	1.12%	

Source: http://ec.europa.eu/budget/figures/2012/2012_en.cfm (retrieved 10 January 2012)

EU Funds Received by Member State (2009)

Country	Amount	% of Gross National Income
Belgium	€5.63 billion	1.66%
Bulgaria	€979 million	2.96%
Czech Republic	€2.95 billion	2.88%
Denmark	€1.33 billion	0.58%
Germany	€11.7 billion	0.48%
Estonia	€716 million	5.35%
Ireland	€1.38 billion	1.04%
Greece	€5.43 billion	2.35%
Spain	€11.6 billion	1.13%
France	€13.6 billion	0.7%
Italy	€9.37 billion	0.63%
Cyprus	€172 million	1.04%
Latvia	€710 million	3.53%
Lithuania	€1.79 billion	6.73%
Luxembourg	€1.45 billion	5.61%
Hungary	€3.57 billion	4.07%
Malta	€71.4 million	1.32%
Netherlands	€1.85 billion	0.33%
Austria	€1.82 billion	0.66%
Poland	€9.25 billion	3.08%
Portugal	€3.72 billion	2.37%
Romania	€2.95 billion	2.6%
Slovenia	€616 million	1.79%
Slovakia	€1.19 billion	1.9%
Finland	€1.21 billion	0.71%
Sweden	€1.45 billion	0.5%
UK	€6.25 billion	0.39%

Source: http://ec.europa.eu/budget/biblio/multimedia/interactive/fundsbymember state/index_en.cfm (retrieved 25 September 2011)

A significant change in the Commission's responsibilities took place in the 1980s with the advent of the single market programme. This meant that a great deal of the Commission's work became focused on ensuring compliance among member states by monitoring the implementation of legislation. Each year since 1997, the Commission publishes a 'single market scoreboard' that ranks all the EU member states in terms of the policies that they still have to implement. When obligations are broken the Commission can issue a 'reasoned opinion' (second stage warning) to the member state, which it is hoped should result in compliance. If this fails then the Commission can take the matter further by pursuing legal proceedings at the Court of Justice. Given the often truculent attitude of member states to EU policies, there are plenty of examples of such referrals. On 14 May 2009 the Commission referred Poland to the Court because of its non-transposition of EU rules prohibiting gender discrimination in access to and supply of goods and services. This took place after a reasoned opinion was issued in 2008. Where member states do not comply with EU legislation, the European Commission is able to impose fines on governments for breaches of EU law.

Scrutiny of national governments also covers central government subsidies to industry and types of state aid, as well as ensuring that governments in the eurozone are maintaining stable economic policies that do not breach the criteria of the single currency. Individual firms can be fined for violating Treaty law (although they have the right to appeal to the Court of Justice). The single market programme also brought about an expansion of the Commission's work into other areas, such as social and economic cohesion as well as providing support to poorer member states in the form of structural funds. Since the introduction of the euro the Commission has also played an important role in monitoring the economic situation in the eurozone as well as offering judgments on the preparedness and readiness of member states to adopt the single currency.

The delegation of such responsibility has also resulted in a growth in the influence and presence of the Commission within and outside the member states. When arguments arise between member states over specific issues it is the Commission that is called upon to assist with reaching an agreement by undertaking a 'mediation role' and also acting as a referee. The Commission also performs a key diplomatic representative role, having over 130 delegations and offices around the world.

COMPETITION BATTLES: MICROSOFT VERSUS THE COMMISSION

From the late 1990s, Microsoft, the world's leading manufacturer of computer software, was engaged in a decade-long dispute with the EU. The dispute centred on the Commission's argument that Microsoft was engaged in anti-competitive practices. The background to this case was that in December 1998 Sun Microsystems complained to the European Commission that Microsoft was refusing to provide it with interoperability information that would allow it to interoperate with Microsoft's PC system, which was the market leader. After a period of investigation, the Commission decided in March 2004 that Microsoft had abused its market position by not providing the interoperability information and by restricting competition by tying the Windows Media Player with the Microsoft PC operating system. In its decision, the Commission required Microsoft to provide interoperability information within a period of 120 days, to offer a version of its Windows PC operating system without Windows Media Player within a period of 90 days, and also to pay a fine of €497 million. While Microsoft inevitably challenged this decision, the Court of First Instance upheld the Commission ruling in September 2007. This then led to the Commission imposing a record fine of €899 million on Microsoft in February 2008, which reflected the 488 days from March 2004 until 22 October 2007 when Microsoft refused to comply with the Commission ruling.

It was not until 16 December 2009 that Microsoft agreed to provide users with a choice of browser, and in so doing brought to an end this long-running dispute. Microsoft was the first company in fifty years of EU competition policy that the Commission had to resort to issuing with a fine because of a failure to comply with a decision on anti-competitive practices.

Criticism

An inevitable consequence of the combination of the significant roles undertaken by the Commission and the fact that the Commissioners are not directly appointed has meant that accountability has long been an important concern with regard to its workings. However, since the 1993 Maastricht Treaty the European Parliament has played a more active supervisory role over the Commission. For example, while the European Council has the task of proposing a candidate to be President of the Commission, the candidate then needs to secure the support of a majority of all Members of the European Parliament. If this is not achieved, the Council of Ministers needs to put forward another candidate within a month. The Parliament also has the responsibility for approving (or not) the collective body of European Commissioners, as well as the ability to force the Commission to resign through a vote of censure.

The Commission has also suffered from problems relating to inefficiencies, scandals and financial mismanagement. This was highlighted by the resignation of the Santer Commission on 15 March 1999 because earlier that day a Committee of Independent Experts published a report entitled *Allegations Regarding Fraud, Mismanagement and Nepotism in the European Commission*. The report, which had been instigated by the European Parliament, highlighted numerous failings by the Commission. One of the most publicly criticised was the decision by the French

Commissioner, Edith Cresson, to employ her dentist as a personal adviser. This obviously raised questions as to how a dentist could advise on European affairs, and the scandal surrounding this and other activities pressurised the Commission to resign after the European Parliament passed a vote of no confidence in the Commission as a whole. Such an outcome was a profound moment in the history of European integration. Not only did it signal the willingness of the European Parliament to use its powers over the Commission, but also it represented a decline in the Commission's power and signalled a tilting of influence towards the Council of Ministers and the European Council.

6

The national interest: the Council of the European Union

The forum where the member state governments meet at a European level to discuss EU issues is known as the Council of the European Union. In crude terms this is where they get together to thrash out deals that they then attempt to portray to their electorates as best representing the national interest. The Council comprises the Council of Ministers, the European Council, the Committee of Permanent Representatives and a plethora of technical committees.

For much of the history of European integration the Council was a forum where member states could represent the national interest. Since the early 1990s this situation has begun to change as a larger body of permanent staff dealing with key policies is to be found in the Council building. Some Eurosceptics regard this as an erosion of the national interest. Yet in the eyes of member state governments this change has been borne out of necessity. The extension of the EU's remit into such areas as foreign and security policy meant that it was difficult to administer these policies purely between the member states alone. In truth, structures had to be created and staff appointed to them.

The most obvious example has been the appointment on 1 December 2009 of the former Belgian Prime Minister, Herman Van Rompuy, as the first President of the European Council (often incorrectly referred to as President of the EU).

The President, who is chosen by the leaders of the EU member states, is appointed for a period of two and half years, with the provision that the appointment can only be renewed once. This new position was deemed crucial because it provided greater continuity to the work of the European Council, which until that time had been led by each member state on a six-month rotating basis.

In tandem with the creation of the post of President of the European Council, agreement was reached to merge the Council's previous responsibility in foreign policy with the Commission's responsibility in external affairs. This resulted in the appointment in October 2008 of Britain's EU Commissioner Baroness Catherine Ashton to the new post of High Representative for Foreign Affairs and Security Policy. As with European Commissioners, the High Representative is appointed for a renewable five-year term. The High Representative occupies a unique position because it is 'double hatted' in that the post serves the Council as well as the Commission. In this sense, Catherine Ashton as High Representative is, along with the leaders of the EU member states, a member of the European Council and at the same time a European Commissioner. The rationale for this dual role is that it provides a unified viewpoint between the work of the Commission and the Council on foreign policy matters.

Council of Ministers

Whereas the Commission is a permanently staffed organisation, the structure of the Council is rather different. On the one hand, it has a permanent staff in the form of the General Secretariat which assists with arranging meeting space, taking minutes, providing policy papers, legal assistance and research services. On the other, the Council is a highly transitory institution, with national ministers and officials who use the Council base in the

Justus Lipsius building as a place to meet and tackle the bulk of the key issues.

The Council of Ministers is a key EU institution because it is the only place that represents the interests of the member states, who are after all the main paymasters and decision-takers in the EU. It is therefore viewed as being one of the most intergovernmental EU institutions, as the decisions that are taken within its walls are for the most part determined by the member states.

In basic terms, the Council of Ministers is where the member states take decisions on EU policies, co-ordinate national policies and resolve differences between themselves and other institutions. In conjunction with the Commission the Council acts as the EU executive, but it also performs a legislative role with the European Parliament through the co-decision procedure. This has made the Council of Ministers and the European Parliament 'co-legislatures'. After the European Commission has put forward a new law or policy, it is the task of the Council of Ministers and the European Parliament to discuss and make changes to the law or policy.

THE COUNCIL OF MINISTERS' ROLE IN INITIATING EU LEGISLATION

The Council receives legislative proposals from the European Commission.

⇓

Proposals are then reviewed by the appropriate Council committees or working parties.

⇓

Proposals are reviewed by the Committee of Permanent Representatives (Coreper).

⇓

Proposals are then sent to the relevant Council of Ministers for discussion.

⇓

Discussion then takes place between the Council of Ministers and the European Parliament through the co-decision procedure.

⇓

Final agreement is reached.

Today the Council has in the vast majority of cases to work in tandem with the European Parliament to reach a decision on these matters. Inevitably each member state has a particular viewpoint that it wishes to advance in these negotiations and the extent to which a government is able to be flexible in its negotiating position is heavily shaped by the domestic political context. What this means in practice is that the Council is a representation forum for national governments, a key decision-making institution, but it is also one of the main negotiating forums in the EU.

The end product of this situation is that although we may conclude that the Council has come to an agreed position, it is evident that rarely do member states share the same preferences. For example, Britain, the Netherlands, Poland and Spain have been strong supporters of the need for the European defence policy to be linked to the United States. By contrast, France, Luxembourg, Belgium and to an extent Germany have been key advocates of the need for the EU to have a defence policy that is independent of America. Yet on other issues, such as budget negotiations, it would be perfectly possible to have a divide between net-contributor nations such as Britain, France and Germany and net-recipient nations such as Spain and Poland. On other issues there might be a left–right ideological divide. So the overall outcome will always be one of compromise that will result in alliances shifting depending on the policy being discussed.

The significance of the Council's role in EU politics has often been cited in retaliation to Eurosceptic critics who argue that too much power has been transferred away from the national level. This argument is considerably more complex. While the Council might still retain substantial influence, the individual role of the member states within the Council is not equal. The Council is itself not without criticism; for instance, it is often noted that there is a lack of transparency and scrutiny with regard to the decisions that it takes.

The expansion in the number of policy areas that are covered by the EU has inevitably brought more and more areas of domestic affairs into the European arena. Thus while in the early years of European integration meetings of the Council were essentially the preserve of a limited number of government ministers, such as foreign affairs, trade, agriculture and finance, today every area of national government has in one way or another some sort of involvement in its meetings. Today it is possible to have Council meetings that do not match domestic portfolios of government ministers. The end result is that some government ministers sometimes have to attend more than one meeting.

There is an unwritten pecking order in the ten different configurations in which the Council of Ministers meets, with the Foreign Affairs Council (comprising Foreign Ministers) and the Economic and Financial Affairs (ECOFIN) Council (comprising Finance Ministers) at the top. Some Council meetings have also become increasingly important in recent years because of the significance and the volume of their work. The most notable example of this is the Justice and Home Affairs Council, as the EU's involvement on matters relating to policy areas such as immigration and border controls has expanded considerably since the end of the Cold War, which broke down boundaries that had restricted movement between many European countries for the previous fifty years.

CONFIGURATIONS OF THE COUNCIL OF MINISTERS, 2011

Agriculture and Fisheries

Competitiveness (includes industry, single market and research policy)

Economic and Financial Affairs (includes co-ordination of economic policy, checking financial health of member states, broader context of financial markets, and economic relations with developing world)

Education, Youth and Culture

Employment, Social Policy, Health and Consumer Affairs (also includes equal opportunities)

Environment

Foreign Affairs (includes Common Foreign and Security Policy (CFSP) and European Security and Defence Policy (ESDP), development co-operation, trade policy)

General Affairs (includes issues that cut across different portfolios such as enlargement and financing agreements, as well as general discussions relating to European Council meetings)

Justice and Home Affairs (includes the area of freedom, security and justice (AFSJ))

Transport, Telecommunications and Energy

The need to ensure that compromise is achieved has been reflected in the move to make more and more use of qualified majority voting (QMV). What this means in practice is that each member state is given a number of votes that are broadly reflective of the population of the country. For the Council to reach agreement all that needs to be achieved is for a number of votes to pass the majority level. Conversely, of course, it is possible for a group of countries to adopt a blocking position that would stop a decision being taken. This is known as the blocking minority. Eurosceptics argue that the shift to QMV is a means of eroding the influence of individual member states.

QMV and the Distribution of Votes in the Council of Ministers, 2012

France, Germany, Italy and the United Kingdom	29
Poland and Spain	27
Romania	14
Netherlands	13
Belgium, Czech Republic, Greece, Hungary and Portugal	12
Austria, Bulgaria and Sweden	10
Denmark, Finland, Ireland, Lithuania, Slovakia	7
Cyprus, Estonia, Latvia, Luxembourg and Slovenia	4
Malta	3
Total	**345**

Note: QMV is reached when a majority of the member states approve and if a minimum of 255 votes are cast in favour (73.9% of the total).

In addition, a member state can ask for clarity as to whether the percentage of votes in favour equals at least 62% of the EU's total population. If it is less than 62% the decision is not adopted.

Presidency of the Council of Ministers

Although the Council could technically be viewed as a reactive institution that waits until it receives a Commission proposal before it engages in the decision-making process, as a collective body the member states do attempt to influence the way in which the direction of European integration progresses. One of the most obvious examples of this has been the six-month term of office when an individual member state assumes the Presidency of the Council. This traditionally provided an opportunity for the leader of a member state government to be responsible for organising the working priorities of the Council of Ministers as well as assuming the role of President of the European Council. These roles conferred a great deal of power and prestige on national leaders. However, with the introduction in 2009 of the 'permanent' position of President of the European Council, there occurred a downgrading in the six-monthly rotating Presidency as the national leader is no longer able to assume the post of President of the Council.

Despite this development, the rotating Presidency position is still of considerable importance as it allows each member state to take charge of the agenda setting of the Council for a six-month period that is divided between January to June and July to December, with there being a strict rota for such tasks. The member state that chairs the Presidency provides it with a key opportunity to raise its profile on the global stage. But the Presidency also provides an important public relations exercise whereby national governments have an opportunity to increase the profile attached to European integration in their own country. On occasion, this can result in rather strange ideas that have diplomatic repercussions. Such was the zeal of Britain's New Labour government to champion European integration in a populist manner when it was elected to office in 1997, that when it chaired the Presidency in 1998 the government decided that its Presidency tie should be designed by a group of schoolchildren, who, somewhat predictably, produced rather stereotypical images of EU member states. No doubt the Italian Prime Minister, Romano Prodi, was none too pleased when he received a tie bearing the image of a pizza.

Rotating Presidency of the EU

Year	January–June	July–December
2000	Portugal	France
2001	Sweden	Belgium
2002	Spain	Denmark
2003	Greece	Italy
2004	Ireland	Netherlands
2005	Luxembourg	United Kingdom
2006	Austria	Finland
2007	Germany	Portugal
2008	Slovenia	France
2009	Czech Republic	Sweden
2010	Spain	Belgium
2011	Hungary	Poland
2012	Denmark	Cyprus
2013	Ireland	Lithuania
2014	Greece	Italy
2015	Latvia	Luxembourg
2016	Netherlands	Slovakia
2017	Malta	United Kingdom
2018	Estonia	Bulgaria
2019	Austria	Romania

The task of chairing the Presidency was straightforward in the early years of European integration. With just six member states the Presidency would rotate swiftly. As the EU has expanded over the years, the role of the Presidency has been subject to greater scrutiny in terms of its effectiveness. In an EU of twenty-seven rather different member states, it is also evident that any member state is only going to assume the Presidency every thirteen and a half years. Thus, whereas France held the Presidency nine times between 1958 and 1989 (in 1959, 1962, 1965, 1968, 1971, 1974, 1979, 1984 and 1989), it is only scheduled to chair the Presidency three times between 1990 and 2019 (in 1995, 2000 and 2008). Moreover, because there are clear distinctions in the size and influence of each member state, ranging from Malta and Luxembourg, which have populations that are smaller than many cities, to the likes of Germany, there are going to be questions about whether it is possible to establish a coherent EU position, particularly in regard to important international issues. Against this background of an enlarged EU membership, an expansion in the number of EU policies and an increasingly complex global environment, there was a need to provide a more stable structure for co-ordinating the foreign policy of the EU.

Speaking with one voice: the President of the European Council

Concern about the lack of a coherent position among the member states on European issues can be traced back to the 1970s when the former US Secretary of State, Henry Kissinger, supposedly commented, 'Who do I call if I want to speak to Europe?' The underlying message that there was a need for Europe to establish a clearer and more united policy at a global level was regularly trotted out by European leaders who wanted to justify the need for ever-closer integration in European foreign policy. Although the years that followed were marked by efforts to achieve such an objective, it was not until the 1997 Treaty of Amsterdam that a post was created which provided a single voice on foreign policy matters, namely the High Representative for the

Common Foreign and Security Policy. A decade later further changes were made in the Treaty of Lisbon, with the appointment of a permanent President of the European Council. But this created a somewhat muddled situation whereby it is possible to have four individuals who can all claim the title of President in a European context. There is the President of the Commission, the President of the European Parliament, the six-month rotating Presidency of the EU, and finally the post of President of the European Council.

The appointment of Herman Van Rompuy as the first President of the European Council also brought into question the extent to which this was a democratic process as the choice of Van Rompuy was the result of backroom deals in smoke-filled rooms by heads of state and government rather than the decision of Europe's electorate. This would result in Nigel Farage, an MEP from the UK Independence Party, savaging Van Rompuy in a debate in the European Parliament on 24 February 2010 when he said, 'I've never heard of you. Nobody in Europe has ever heard of you. Who voted for you?'

HERMAN VAN ROMPUY

On 19 November 2009 Herman Van Rompuy (b.1947) was elected by the leaders of EU member states to serve as the first permanent President of the European Council for a period of two and a half years (renewable once). He took up his position on 1 January 2010. Prior to his appointment he had served as Prime Minister of Belgium since December 2008. Van Rompuy was a compromise candidate after the initial front-runner for the post, former British Prime Minister Tony Blair, failed to achieve the support of EU leaders. This was primarily because of Blair's support for the invasion of Iraq, which created divisions between EU member states. There was initially a considerable amount of concern over Van Rompuy's

> appointment as he was not regarded as a 'big hitter' who would be able to stamp his authority on the post. No doubt some member states viewed this as an advantage, however, as it would enable them to continue to exercise national influence over European foreign policy.

Despite the move to strengthen European co-operation through the creation of the post of EU President, individual national Presidencies still continue to be important in terms of organising much of the day-to-day work of the Council, as well as in terms of brokering compromise between the member states. And while the member state that chairs the Presidency of the Council of Ministers will have a particular set of issues that it wishes to pursue, it nonetheless does have to be careful to ensure that it also charts a course that is representative of the broader European interest. If it does not, the results can be disastrous. Clearly the task of organising the activity of the Council and of trying to bring coherence to such a large group of diverse countries is not for the faint-hearted. It places significant demands on the administrative skills of the individuals and countries concerned.

European Council

The European Council comprises heads of state and government and was established in 1975 after a number of 'fireside chats' among the leaders of the member states produced a conclusion that there was a real need for the very top levels of government to get together on more than just an ad hoc basis. The value of such 'summit' meetings had been evident since President Georges Pompidou of France had called for a special meeting of the six member states to be held at The Hague in December 1969 in order to 'relaunch' the Community. Although in the period after 1969 several occasional summits took place, such as in Paris in 1972, the first formal European Council took place in Dublin in March 1975. Since that first Dublin meeting, the European Council has played an important role in the development of European integration through giving political direction, establishing priorities and resolving disputes.

Key Meetings of the European Council

Date	Venue	Issue
1–2 December 1969	The Hague	Relaunch of the Community
10–11 March 1975	Dublin	First formal meeting of the Council
6–7 July 1978	Bremen	Creation of the European Monetary System
25–6 June 1984	Fontainebleau	Agreement on a British budget rebate
2–3 December 1985	Luxembourg	Agreement on the Single European Act
9–10 December 1991	Maastricht	Agreement on the Treaty on European Union (Maastricht Treaty)
21–2 June 1993	Copenhagen	Establishment of enlargement criteria for countries from Central and Eastern Europe
16–17 June 1997	Amsterdam	Agreement on the Treaty of Amsterdam
23–4 March 2000	Lisbon	Agreement on the Lisbon Strategy for economic competitiveness

Cont'd

Date	Venue	Issue
7–9 December 2000	Nice	Agreement on the Treaty of Nice
17–18 June 2004	Brussels	Agreement on a European Constitution
13 December 2007	Lisbon	Agreement on the Treaty of Lisbon
23–4 June 2011	Brussels	Discussion on eurozone debt crisis
26 October 2011	Brussels	Crisis summit on eurozone
8–9 December 2011	Brussels	Agreement on short-term action to overcome the debt crisis and a new fiscal compact for the eurozone

At a minimum, there are two European Council meetings each year, in June and December, and, apart from anything else, they are used as a means of bringing to an end the work of the member state that has chaired the Presidency. There can be more meetings, sometimes up to four in a year. While the key end of Presidency European Council meetings have always been high-profile events that take place in key locations within the member state holding the Presidency, others have taken place in Brussels. On rare occasions it is necessary for the EU heads of state and government to meet to discuss urgent matters in a European Council format. For instance, in the wake of the terrorist attacks on the United States on 11 September 2001 there was an emergency European Council meeting in Brussels on 21 September to discuss the EU's response.

The razzmatazz of European diplomacy

Whereas the regular meetings of the Council of Ministers barely register with the public and are often ignored by the media, European Council meetings are a full-blown glitzy affair. Often they are concerned with resolving the most intractable problems or trying to broker compromises on new policy developments. Key policy decisions are often associated with where the European Council meeting took place. The resolution of Britain's budget contribution is inextricably linked to the outcome that was achieved at the 1984 Fontainebleau European Council. When a European Council has reached agreement on a Treaty reform, that Treaty has often been named after the location of the meeting. Recent Treaty reform that emerged out of the Constitutional Treaty negotiations is now known as the Lisbon Treaty. Before that we had the Nice Treaty, the Amsterdam Treaty and the Maastricht Treaty. What is particularly important about the European Council is that it offers a forum that facilitates a better understanding of issues among the national leaders. It also provides a vehicle whereby important goals can be identified, such as the establishment of the single market and the creation of a single currency. It is a meeting of last resort for those issues that could not be agreed at the Council of Ministers and/or which were unsuitable for their discussion. The Council also provides an opportunity to drive policy forward and reach agreement on issues that can only be resolved at head of state and government level. Such issues, such as agreement on the single currency or closer co-operation on foreign affairs, can really only be taken at this level because of the implications that they have on the sovereignty of member states.

Meetings of the European Council are often tense, fraught affairs. This is hardly surprising as leaders of member states are well used to getting their own way. The growth in the number of member states has meant that round-table forums for conducting negotiations are not always the most conducive to obtaining an agreement. Apart from anything else, a very brief one-minute *tour de table* introduction and hello by each leader would take at least half an hour. So how are agreements established? The answer is that there is a great deal of preparatory work, with heads of state and government and other key ministers engaging in shuttle diplomacy to meet with government ministers in other member states before each European Council meeting. Such visits are important to the construction of alliances. It is where deals are struck. This can range from trying to garner support for a new policy proposal to establishing groupings of member states that have sufficient weight to block a proposal. When the European Council eventually takes place, this format of informal diplomacy is mirrored in the fact that much of the work takes place in the corridors and over a coffee (or something stronger) in the various bars and coffee lounges that are scattered around the Council building. Wherever the discussions take place, it is still the case that if the heads of state and government do not like an idea then it is basically finished.

Permanent Representations

All the work that is undertaken in the European Council and the Council of Ministers cannot solely be dealt with from the government ministries and officials based in the national capital. Each member state requires a base in Brussels that acts as the representative office of that country. Known as Permanent Representations, each is staffed by a broad range of officials who have expert knowledge of the EU and are able to reflect the interests of government departments in the national capital. An inevitable consequence of the gradual expansion in the number of policies that are dealt with at the EU level is that there has been a growth in the number of staff based in Permanent Representations.

These staff spend the majority of their time participating in meetings in the Council of Ministers, where their task is to defend the interests of their member state government. The regular meetings that the staff attend with their counterparts from other member state Permanent Representations are known as working groups. The work that is conducted in these groups can vary from looking at the drafting of detailed policy to discussing a response to events. As such, staff act as the local 'eyes and ears' of the member state government: their task goes beyond following the instructions of government ministers to providing crucial advice that helps to shape government policy. Even the Belgian government has a Brussels-based Permanent Representation to the EU.

This representative and negotiating role is therefore different from, say, the work of an Embassy to another country, whose primary focus is purely of a representative nature. The constant nature and the political sensitivity of the work in which Permanent Representations get involved require a senior and suitably skilled negotiator to be in charge. Such an individual is known as the Permanent Representative, invariably a senior member of the Foreign Office of a member state.

Permanent Representations expend their greatest effort by lobbying and negotiating on behalf of national capitals and informing the latter of the extent to which EU activities affect them. One of their most important tasks is to gather and provide information for governments as to what proposals are being raised in Brussels, such as by the European Commission. Other tasks include those of policy formulation (by assisting in putting together national policy towards EU issues and proposals) and that of negotiator (by taking part in the many committee meetings that hammer out EU policy). Officials from Permanent Representations also offer advice to government ministers during the various ministerial discussions, varying from agricultural policy to foreign affairs.

Permanent Representations consequently play a significant and important role in the EU policy-making process by acting as the link between domestic capitals and the EU institutions. The crucial factor that distinguishes Permanent Representations from other forms of diplomacy, such as that of an Embassy, is the constant engagement in the negotiating process.

Representing the national interest?

The Council of Ministers and the European Council play an important role in the EU because they act as a means of linking national governments to the decision-making structure. This is of extreme importance in demonstrating to national electorates that their governments are able to represent their interests in the EU. Because it is impossible to reach agreement on a basis where every member state government has to agree to a policy pro-posal, there has been a shift to decisions being taken on a quali-fied majority voting basis in the Council of Ministers. This means that governments cannot always achieve outcomes that reflect their interests. This leads to a tricky situation whereby national electorates, political parties and other relevant lobby groups crit-icise governments for being ineffective in defending the national position. Such criticism ignores the fact that at its core the EU is a grouping of member states who have come together to tackle common issues where the reaching of common agreement requires compromise.

7

The people's voice: the European Parliament

Of all the EU institutions, the European Parliament has changed the greatest in the course of the history of European integration. That change has been particularly marked since the early 1990s when the European Parliament gained more influence and power in the decision-making structure through the co-decision procedure that was introduced in the Maastricht Treaty. But despite this augmentation in its power, the European Parliament does not register among national electorates as a significant institution. There are a number of reasons for this. Members of the European Parliament (MEPs) are elected by citizens who essentially cast their vote on the basis of national politics. Once elected, MEPs are grouped into transnational political alliances that range from the Eurosceptic to the most federalist. The largest political grouping is the one that is dominant in the Parliament. These political groupings do not accurately reflect national or European viewpoints. An inevitable consequence of this is that it is hard for national electorates to connect with the work of the Parliament. Very few members of the public would be able to name MEPs in the way that they can name their national parliamentarians. All of this is borne out in the fact that elections to the European Parliament generally have a lower voter turnout than national elections.

A timid start

The European Parliament's origins can be traced to the creation of the European Coal and Steel Community (ECSC) in 1952. At that time it was merely referred to as the Parliamentary Assembly and many of the struggles over recent decades to increase the power of the Parliament rest in the fact that the founding fathers of European integration paid only lip service to providing the initial institutions with a democratic structure. For them the key issue was the creation of strong executive bodies in the form of the High Authority of the ECSC (now the European Commission) and the Council of Ministers. By contrast, the Parliamentary Assembly was there to provide some political advice and its low status was confirmed by the fact that provision did not even exist for directly elected representatives in the early years.

When the European Community was formally established on 1 January 1958 by the Treaty of Rome, the Parliamentary Assembly was given relatively little power to exercise control or influence over the other institutions. It was only able to issue non-binding opinions on policies being proposed by the European Commission. In practice, this meant that the European Commission and the Council of Ministers could ignore the Assembly (known as the Parliament from 1962). And as the Parliament had a negligible influence on the decision-making process within the Community, it was unsurprising that it was not taken seriously by other bodies, organisations and the media, as well as the general public.

Many commentators would reflect that the debates that took place within the Parliament were pointless. For them the Parliament was not much more than a talking shop. Its powers were limited, having little ability to persuade either the Commission or the Council to take into account its views. The weak and unelected nature of the European Parliament did, however, produce a backlash as many groups were critical of the way in which it had been marginalised in the institutional structure to being an ad hoc adviser. This quickly became known as a democratic deficit.

To remedy this situation it was decided in the mid-1970s that the Parliament should be directly elected for the first time in 1979. MEPs were to serve five-year terms. Elections have subsequently taken place in either a year ending with a 4 or a 9. But while direct elections partly brought a change to the Parliament's status, with the 1980s witnessing an increase in its power and influence, it was not until the 1993 Maastricht Treaty that its influence really began to change. At Maastricht, the member state governments decided to introduce what became known as the co-decision procedure, which instantly transformed the Parliament's role. As its name suggests, the co-decision procedure meant that the Parliament would in effect become a joint decision-maker with the Council.

The post-Maastricht years witnessed a steady growth in the Parliament's powers, and it was the institution that tended to gain the most influence out of EU negotiations that resulted in Treaty changes. Indeed, as the EU developed a fondness for Treaty change, there has been quite a significant change to the Parliament's influence since the early 1990s. Most recently the 2009 Treaty of Lisbon extended the scope of the co-decision procedure to forty new policy areas. Co-decision is now known as the ordinary legislative procedure in the EU. It covers the majority of policy areas, including: agriculture, asylum, combating discrimination, consumer affairs, culture, economic and social cohesion, energy services, environment, fisheries, free movement of workers, industrial support measures, single market, immigration, justice and home affairs, public health, research, social exclusion, trans-European networks and visas.

Moreover, the expansion of the co-decision procedure to areas such as justice and home affairs illustrates the way in which policies that were once solely the preserve of the decision making of the member states have required stronger and more effective policies to be established at a European level. The Parliament's power is, however, not just limited to involvement in legislative procedures; in recent years it has been more active in flexing its muscles by scrutinising the EU institutions, particularly the European Commission.

How does the European Parliament work?

The fact that the European Parliament is directly elected and has influence over EU policy-making might lead you to consider that it is comparable to national parliaments. One obvious difference is the fact that the current number of 736 MEPs do not sit in national delegations, but instead sit in Europe-wide political groupings. In the seventh Parliamentary term, which commenced in 2009, there were seven political groups.

As the EU has expanded there has been a need to readjust the number of MEPs that are allocated to each member state because otherwise there would just not be enough space in the Parliament. The current total of 736 MEPs who were elected in June 2009 was set out in the Treaty of Nice, although the recent Treaty of Lisbon has provided a slight increase in the number of MEPs to 751 from the next European Parliament elections in 2014.

When the Parliament meets in plenary session, MEPs sit in political groupings within a chamber where seats are arranged in a horseshoe fashion. While this arrangement is typical of many parliaments, it is different from the UK model in the House of Commons where the arrangement of government and opposition benches often leads to heated debate. But as with other

Membership of Political Groups in the European Parliament, Seventh Parliamentary Term, 2009–14 (as of October 2011)

Group	No. of MEPs
Group of the European People's Party (Christian Democrats)	265
Group of the Progressive Alliance of Socialists and Democrats in the European Parliament	184
Group of the Alliance of Liberals and Democrats for Europe	85
Group of the Greens/European Free Alliance	55
European Conservatives and Reformists Group	54
Confederal Group of the European United Left/ Nordic Green Left	35
Europe of Freedom and Democracy Group	30
Non-aligned	28
Total	**736**

parliaments around the world, much of the work of the European Parliament is undertaken in committees, while there are also groups that focus on such issues as animal rights.

A key question is how the European Parliament should develop in the future. Whereas some believe that it should maintain a model of operation whose primary role is to offer a democratic counterweight to the other EU institutions, others consider that its powers should be further strengthened. This debate can be divided into two camps. The first is that the Parliament's role should be strengthened to such an extent that it operates in way that is reflective of a national parliament, albeit at a European level. Such an argument would inevitably lead to a downgrading in the role of national parliaments as more and more business gets dealt with at a European level. The reality of such an outcome is rather slim given the fact that few (if any) member states would want to dilute the influence of their own national parliaments. Moreover, there would inevitably be concerns about the extent to which transnational political groupings in the Parliament could actually enhance a sense of democratic ownership of the process by the local electorate. Indeed, it is worth remembering that the Parliament is itself a unique experiment: there is no other example of a multinational directly elected Parliament in the world. In contrast to this view, the second camp argues that the primary democratic link is and should continue to be one in which national parliaments control their governments, which in turn represent the member states in the Council of Ministers. There are considerable merits to such an argument, not least the fact that the electorate in member states still find it hard to relate to what can only be described as some of the rather bizarre operating methods of the Parliament.

MEPs AND EUROPEAN PARLIAMENT ELECTIONS

Once elected, MEPs join alliances with other MEPs who share similar political views. In the case of the UK, MEPs who are elected under the banner of the Labour Party form part of the Party of European Socialists within the European Parliament. In a similar manner German Christian Democrat MEPs form part of the European People's Party Group. This is significant because it highlights the transnational nature of the political groupings within the European Parliament, whereby MEPs are supposed to reflect political and not national priorities. European Parliament elections are, however, influenced by national politics and are generally regarded as an important test of the level of support for member state governments. In some instances, the elections can be used as a form of protest vote against the government of the day.

The European Parliament's shuttle

The most obvious example of the strange working methods of the European Parliament is that it actually has three places of work. The administrative offices of the Parliament are located in Luxembourg, and the majority of the meetings of the whole Parliament (known as plenary sessions) take place in Brussels. This is where the political parties meet and where the committees do their work by reviewing legislation. However, the MEPs do not actually vote in the Parliament building in Brussels. Rather, once a month the Parliament moves 216 miles south to the French city of Strasbourg on the historic fault line between France and Germany. And while the MEPs meet in Strasbourg for just forty-eight days each year, this is where they take their decisions.

You may wonder why this ludicrous situation has occurred and many people would point the finger of excess and wastefulness at the MEPs themselves. Yet the decision for this state of affairs was actually taken by the member state governments in the Treaty of Maastricht. What this means in practice is that it is the equivalent of the British Parliament relocating every month to Birmingham or Glasgow or the German Bundestag relocating to Frankfurt or Hamburg. The cost of moving the European Parliament to Strasbourg is huge and has resulted in the shuttle between Brussels and Strasbourg being given the unfortunate nickname the 'travelling circus'.

MORE THAN A TRAVELLING CIRCUS?

To understand why the European Parliament's meetings take place in Brussels and Strasbourg each month, we have to go back to the foundation of the ECSC in 1952, whose institutions were based in Luxembourg. At that time the Council of Europe had already been established in Strasbourg to provide a forum for intergovernmental co-operation after the Second World War and it offered its rooms as a meeting place for the Common Assembly of the ECSC, which in 1962 became known as the European Parliament. When the European Economic Community began operating in 1958, the majority of its work was conducted in Brussels, albeit with the Parliament continuing to be located in Strasbourg. The years that followed saw an increase in the Parliament's powers of scrutiny and so there was a gravitational pull towards Brussels. In the early 1990s Belgium supported the building of new offices for the Parliament in Brussels and at the same time France supported the construction of a new Parliament building in Strasbourg. Both countries were as keen as mustard for the Parliament to have a base in their nation, although the practical realities were that Brussels was the logical location. To placate France and as a measure of the crazy deals that can come out of EU negotiations, heads of state and government agreed in the Maastricht Treaty to retain Strasbourg as a formal meeting place for the Parliament.

The implication of this arrangement is that there is a substantial economic cost in the movement between Brussels and Strasbourg, while environmental campaigners point to the cost in terms of carbon footprint. The latest estimates from the European Parliament indicate that each of the twelve plenary sessions that take place in Brussels costs €10 million. This is to cover the cost of the movement of 736 MEPs, nearly two thousand administrative staff, and the dozen-plus lorries transporting the necessary files and documents. In addition, lobbyists, journalists, diplomats and representatives of other EU institutions such as the Commission travel to Strasbourg.

Power and influence

Turning to the powers of the European Parliament, it is possible to outline three main functions. First, it has a legislative role as, alongside the Council of Ministers, it has the responsibility for passing European laws through the co-decision procedure. In the 2004–9 term the Parliament amended and voted on 483 co-decision texts. Second, it has a supervisory role whereby it keeps a watching eye over the other EU institutions, in particular the Commission where it has responsibility for confirming the appointment of the Commission. Third, the Parliament is able to influence the way in which the EU spends its resources as it has a joint responsibility with the Council over the EU budget. This so-called power of the purse means that the Parliament is able to reject a budget if it sees fit.

In addition, the Parliament appoints an Ombudsman empowered to receive complaints from Union citizens concerning maladministration in the activities of the Community institutions or bodies. It can also set up temporary committees of inquiry, whose powers are not confined to examining the actions of the Community institutions but may also relate to actions by member states in implementing Community policies.

In terms of the Parliament's relationship with other EU institutions, it has a limited scrutiny role over the Council of Ministers, with each of the member states that chair the rotating Presidency having to present their programme of work to the Parliament at the start of the Presidency and to account for the work programme at the end. While this area of scrutiny over the Council's work is, to all intents and purposes, merely sabre rattling with little in the way of formal implications, the same cannot be said of the Parliament's relationship with the European Commission.

The Parliament's supervisory role over the appointment of the Commission also gives it the power to force the Commission as a whole to resign by means of a 'motion of censure'. Although the Parliament has never sacked the Commission, the voluntary resignation of the Santer Commission in 1999 was the product of pressure exerted on it by MEPs. To some observers this supervisory role is similar to that undertaken by national parliaments. Crucially, however, whereas national parliaments have a single executive to bring to account, the same cannot be said within the EU.

Voter apathy

Today there are 736 MEPs in twenty-seven member states who are directly elected for a five-year term of office from each member state, with the number of national MEPs being in proportion to population. But while this has resulted in Germany being at one end of the spectrum with ninety-nine MEPs and Malta at the other with five, the situation is reversed when the number of electors per MEP is taken into consideration. Thus, whereas there are approximately eighty thousand voters per MEP in Malta, there are some eight hundred and eighty thousand voters per MEP in France. In other words, Malta has more MEPs per head of population, which further emphasises the lack of uniformity of elections to the European Parliament.

European Parliament Representation

Country	Population (millions)	Fifth term 1999–2004	Sixth term 2004–9	Seventh term 2009–14	Population per MEP (millions)
Germany	82.4	99	99	99	0.83
France	64.057	87	78	72	0.88
Britain	60.776	87	78	72	0.84
Italy	58.147	87	78	72	0.80

Cont'd

Country	Population (millions)	Fifth term 1999–2004	Sixth term 2004–9	Seventh term 2009–14	Population per MEP (millions)
Spain	40.448	64	54	50	0.80
Poland	38.518	0	54	50	0.77
Romania	22.276	0	0	33	0.67
Netherlands	16.570	31	27	25	0.66
Greece	10.706	25	24	22	0.48
Czech Republic	10.288	0	24	22	0.46
Belgium	10.392	25	24	22	0.47
Hungary	9.956	0	24	22	0.45
Portugal	10.642	25	24	22	0.48
Sweden	9.031	22	19	18	0.50
Austria	8.199	21	18	17	0.48
Bulgaria	7.322	0	0	17	0.43
Slovakia	5.477	0	14	13	0.42
Denmark	5.468	16	14	13	0.42
Finland	5.238	16	14	13	0.40
Ireland	4.109	15	13	12	0.34
Lithuania	3.575	0	13	12	0.29
Latvia	2.254	0	9	8	0.65
Slovenia	2.009	0	7	7	0.28
Estonia	1.315	0	6	6	0.21
Cyprus	0.788	0	6	6	0.13
Luxembourg	0.480	6	6	6	0.08
Malta	0.401	0	5	5	0.08
Totals	**497**	**626**	**732**	**736**	
	27 countries	15 countries	25 countries	27 countries	27 countries

The expansion in the size of the European Parliament and the growth in its powers have not had a dramatic impact on voter turnout in European Parliament elections. As is illustrated in the table below, at the last elections in 2009 the average level of voting fell for the sixth time running. As might be expected, there are significant variations between the voting records in different member states. Some countries have a sturdier commitment to Europe and this partly accounts for the strong voter turnout in Belgium, Italy and Luxembourg. By contrast, Britain has traditionally had one of the lowest voter turnouts in European Parliament elections, although an interesting development in the latest elections was the low turnout in a number of the new member states, such as Lithuania and the Czech Republic.

In looking at these issues in more detail, it is important to note that a high voter turnout for some countries is hardly surprising. For some nations, such as Belgium and Luxembourg, the presence of EU institutions is a major boost to their national economy. Voting is also compulsory in both of these countries. A high turnout in Italian elections can partly be explained by the public's desire to gain external legitimacy through the EU for a country that has suffered from a succession of weak (and corrupt) domestic governments. But these countries are, of course, the exception and as such do not help us to understand why there is a general trend to a decline in voter turnout.

To understand this issue, it is worth reminding ourselves that European elections are totally different to any other type of election that we can imagine. If we take the example of local and national elections, it is the case that these elections are about local and national issues. The crucial distinction is that European Parliament elections really have nothing to do with European issues. Members of the European Parliament are without exception elected on the basis of the national context and not the European. Moreover, the debates put forward by the political parties are invariably about national issues. This is despite the fact that MEPs sit within transnational political groupings that have nothing to do with national issues. In this sense, we could argue that European elections are best referred to as the 'dialogue of the deaf'. Candidates tend to stand for election on national issues and the electorate tend to register their vote depending on the success of national governments rather than the European integration process. This is further influenced by the fact that European elections often take place midway through the lifetime of national parliaments. One further problem with European elections is that they are often used as a sounding board for discontent with national governments and as such it is often the case that relatively small parties, such as the Greens, will do better in a European election than they would otherwise do in a national election.

European issues continue to be low on the radar of the national electorate, who often are most concerned about local issues such as employment, schools, hospitals and crime. And while EU legislation does impact on many of these areas of policy, for the most part the electorate tends to view its national politicians as the ones who are accountable.

Voter Turnout in European Parliament Elections

State	1979	1984	1989	1994	1999	2004	2009
Belgium	91.36	92.09	90.73	90.66	91.05	90.81	90.39
Denmark	47.82	52.38	46.17	52.92	50.46	47.89	59.54
Germany	65.73	56.76	62.28	60.02	45.19	43	43.3
Ireland	63.61	47.56	68.28	43.98	50.21	58.58	58.64
France	60.71	56.72	48.8	52.71	46.76	42.76	40.63
Italy	85.65	82.47	81.07	73.6	69.76	71.72	65.05
Luxembourg	88.91	88.79	87.39	88.55	87.27	91.35	90.75
Netherlands	58.12	50.88	47.48	36.69	30.02	39.26	36.75
UK	32.35	32.57	36.37	36.43	24.0	38.52	34.7

Cont'd

State	1979	1984	1989	1994	1999	2004	2009
Greece		80.59	80.03	73.18	70.25	63.22	52.61
Spain			54.71	59.14	63.05	45.14	44.9
Portugal			51.1	35.54	39.93	38.6	36.78
Sweden					38.84	37.85	45.53
Austria					49.4	42.43	45.97
Finland					30.14	39.43	40.3
Czech Republic						28.3	28.2
Estonia						26.38	43.9
Cyprus						72.5	59.4
Lithuania						48.38	20.98
Latvia						41.34	53.7
Hungary						38.5	36.31
Malta						82.39	78.79
Poland						20.87	24.53
Slovenia						28.35	28.33
Slovakia						16.97	19.64
Bulgaria							38.99
Romania							47.67
EU total	61.99	58.98	58.41	56.67	49.51	45.47	43

Source: http://www.europarl.europa.eu/parliament/archive/elections2009/en/turnout_en.html

Although the European Parliament has been viewed as an important mechanism for holding other EU institutions to account, such as the Santer Commission in 1999, which was accused of fraud, the Parliament has itself not been without criticism. Media reports on the Parliament have often referred to it as a 'gravy train', inferring that MEPs fiddled expenses. This was confirmed in 2008 when the existence of a hitherto secret report from 2006 on the audit of 160 MEPs' expenses was leaked to the media. The report, which was prepared by the European Parliament's head of internal audit, Robert Galvin, revealed a systematic abuse of expenses, with some MEPs claiming over €1 million in what were supposed to be business and staff expenses during their period in office. Other MEPs granted themselves bonuses that were greater than 150% of their salary. In total, it was reported that in excess of €100 million could not be accounted for.

But despite the widespread knowledge of the report's existence, the European Parliament refused to publish it officially, resulting in significant criticism over the lack of transparency. The background to the expenses scandal can be traced to the fact that MEPs had traditionally been paid salaries that were set at the same level as national parliamentarians. This inevitably caused considerable discrepancies and resulted in many MEPs using the expenses system as a means of supplementing their income on a regular basis. To the public at large, this obviously causes mistrust in public office.

In an effort to tackle this system reforms were introduced in 2009 so that all MEPs would receive the same fixed salary. This was set at 38.5% of the basic salary of a European Court of Justice Judge. In 2010 this amounted to €7,807.12 a month before EU tax and €6,083.91 a month post-tax. In the UK context this is considerably more than MPs are paid. In addition, MEPs are paid a so-called subsistence allowance of €298 a day to cover hotel bills and meals and all they have to do to get this payment is to sign the attendance registrar.

A democratic balance to the EU?

A crucial question that needs to be asked is whether change in the Parliament's influence is a good thing and whether there has actually been a significant effort to tackle the democratic deficit in the EU. At first glance, many individuals would rightly be concerned that the growth in the Parliament's powers signals a transfer of power and sovereignty away from the national level of the member state and moreover to a group of MEPs that for the most part are unknown to voters. Such criticism is on balance too harsh.

This is because the institutional structure of the EU requires the need for a strong Parliament and MEPs are the only people with an EU salary who are directly elected and therefore account-able to their citizens. Issues of voter apathy and broader national scepticism towards the EU are, as is pointed out elsewhere in this book, greatly influenced by member state governments, which could do a lot more to provide a full and frank debate about the EU within their country. We also need to remind ourselves that despite the expansion in the EU's policies and the strengthening of the Parliament's powers, there nonetheless remain significant areas of policy-making that are the preserve of the member state and for which the parliamentarians elected at the national level are accountable. Nevertheless, there continues to remain con-cerns about democracy within the EU and this has led some commentators to quip that if the EU applied to join the EU it would not be admitted on the grounds that it does not meet its own standards for democracy.

8

The scales of justice: the European Court of Justice

At first glance it could be said that the European Court of Justice (ECJ) has changed the least out of all the EU institutions. As a result the ECJ's role has often been overshadowed by the attention given to the changing fortunes of the European Commission, the increased powers attached to the European Parliament, and the way that the work of the Council has been shaped by modern diplomacy. Despite the lack of attention given to the ECJ, it is nonetheless evident that it plays a crucial role within the EU. The ECJ has a vital task of ensuring the accurate implementation of the terms of the EU Treaties, where its judgments have had a profound impact on shaping and reshaping the landscape of European integration. As a result the ECJ has evolved into one of the most supranational EU institutions.

History

One of the elements that make the EU unique is the fact that there exists a Court of Justice that makes European law. The legal judgments of the ECJ have a direct effect on the member states and have primacy over national law. In other words, the ECJ's judgments have the ability to overturn national judgments and require the parties to whom the judgments apply to implement them.

To understand these issues fully we need to go back to the origins of European integration. The history of the ECJ can be traced back to the founding in 1952 of the European Coal and Steel Community (ECSC) when its role was to protect the terms of the Treaty of Paris, which established the ECSC. This was to be achieved by means of the fact that the decisions taken by the ECSC High Authority were of a legal nature, particularly with regard to their impact on the member states and the coal and steel authorities within them. With the signing of the Treaty of Rome in March 1957 and the creation of the European Communities on 1 January 1958, the ECSC evolved into the ECJ.

At that time the founding fathers were absolutely clear that there was a need to break down the barriers between countries so as to foster closer integration and thereby create the necessary conditions for economic and political stability to flourish. As has already been noted, the requirements of membership were set out in the founding Treaty texts, which in turn created a legal obligation on the member states that noted the requirement for joint decision making, and thereby the surrender of an element of their sovereignty. A consequence of this was that from the very outset of the European project there was a practical need for the ECJ to exist so as to offer judgment on the Treaty texts, which would inevitably be subject to challenges from individuals, companies and member states.

Although the ECJ had a fairly small workload in the early years of European integration, it was nonetheless still able to offer judgments that had a significant impact on the direction of European integration. This particularly applied to the concepts of 'direct effect' and 'primacy' of EU law. Direct effect refers to the provision that EU law is directly applicable in member states and that EU law can be called upon whether a national law exists or not. Primacy of EU law refers to the way in which EU law has superiority over national law in the areas of policy for which the EU holds responsibility.

In 1963 the ECJ established the principle of direct effect of EU law in its judgment of *Van Gend en Loos* v. *Nederlandse Administratie der Belastingen* (Case 26/62). In this case, the transport company *Van Gend en Loos* claimed that the Dutch government had increased the duty that it charged on the importation of chemical goods from Germany since the Treaty of Rome had come into effect in 1957. As such, the company argued that the increase in the national import duty was contradictory to Community legislation. In its judgment, the ECJ set out one of its most important rulings when it stressed that the Community represented a new legal order that both provided rights to individuals and set out obligations. This became known as the principle of direct effect, whereby the rights created by the Community have to be protected by national courts. The outcome was a decision that confirmed the binding nature of Community law, with member states being required to implement the law within their legal system.

One year later in 1964 the primacy of Community law over national law was established in the ECJ's judgment in the case of *Flaminio Costa* v. *ENEL*. Costa was an Italian citizen who had owned shares in an electricity company that was nationalised in 1962, thereby becoming part of the newly created National Electricity Board (ENEL). As a result of this Costa refused to pay his electricity bill based on his argument that he had been adversely affected by nationalisation, which contradicted the essence of the Treaty of Rome. The ECJ was asked by the Italian Constitutional Court to establish whether an Italian law concerning the nationalisation of the production and distribution of electrical energy was compatible with the provisions set out in the Community Treaty. In its judgment the ECJ noted that the 'the law stemming from the Treaty ... (cannot) be overridden by domestic legal provisions', and in so doing established the principle of the primacy of Community law over domestic law. This point was further clarified in the 1978 case of *Simmenthal* v. *Commission*, which noted the supremacy of EU law over national law in a judgment that stated that national courts have to 'apply Community law in its entirety... setting aside any provision of national law which may conflict with it'.

Having established the principles of direct effect and primacy, a number of years later the ECJ established that member states could be held liable for their failure to fulfil Treaty obligations in the 1991 landmark case of *Francovich and Others*. In this case, two Italian citizens who were due pay from an insolvent company argued that the Italian state had been negligent in not implementing Community provisions that protected employees in a case of insolvency. This led the ECJ to establish a key ruling that a state could be held liable and as such created the potential for individuals to claim damages against the state.

Not only did these cases establish the principles of direct effect, they also established the foundations that were essential for market integration to take place. The issue of fair market access was something that the Community had established as a goal from the outset, with the objective of creating a Customs Union being reached in 1968. The significance of this was that it dispensed with the tariff barriers between the member states and at the same time established a common external tariff so as to ensure that one government could not adjust its import duties for the benefit of trade over another member state. Although such measures were perfectly sensible, in reality the member state governments had developed devious strategies to protect their own industries from the competition of other member states. This principally took the form of so-called non-tariff barriers to trade, whereby governments would set out specific standards that stymied competitiveness. Examples included restrictions on product labelling and standards classifications protecting domestic products.

While this strategy may have had benefits in terms of protecting local employment, it had a deleterious impact on the overall
competitiveness of the Community, a situation that was particularly apparent in the 1970s. Once again, it would be the ECJ that
brought a key issue to a head in the 1979 *Cassis de Dijon* ruling,
which tackled a German ban on the importation of alcoholic
beverages from other member states that did not meet minimum
German alcohol contents. In responding to this situation, the
ECJ ruled that 'There is therefore no valid reason why, provided
that they have been lawfully produced and marketed in one of
the Member States, alcoholic beverages should not be introduced
into any other Member State: the sale of such products may not
be subject to a legal prohibition on the marketing of beverages
with an alcohol content lower than the limit set by the national
rules.'

Despite the significance of this ruling, wholesale change in
terms of tackling the various obstructions that hampered full
market access would not be undertaken until the single market
programme that was agreed to in the 1987 Single European Act.
This was because although rulings such as that of *Cassis de Dijon*
were significant, they represented just the tip of the iceberg and
the ECJ's ability to tackle these issues was wholly dependent on
cases being lodged with it. Thus, when Community leaders
finally agreed on a single market programme, including the measures that would be necessary to achieve the free movement of
people, persons, services and capital, it was not surprising that the
workload of the ECJ increased dramatically.

In examining the history of the European Court of Justice,
one of the most striking factors is that there has been an inherent
tendency for it to offer judgments that have favoured deeper
integration rather than a return of power to the member state
level. This has led to many academic scholars questioning whether
it is possible to regard the Court as a neutral body. Thus, studies
have routinely made reference to the Court being 'integrationist'

and 'activist' in relation to the judgments that it has passed. Indeed, some scholars would go so far as to argue that, when compared to all the other EU institutions, the ECJ has done more and gone further to advance the cause of European integration.

Role

Based in Luxembourg, the ECJ comprises twenty-seven judges from each of the twenty-seven member states. One judge is selected to be President for a three-year renewable term. The structure of the Court has been designed to ensure that all the national legal systems are represented. The Court rarely sits with all twenty-seven judges present; instead the majority of its work is conducted in either a 'Grand Chamber' of thirteen judges or in smaller chambers of three or five judges. The Court additionally receives the support of eight Advocates General. They are Court officers whose role is to give preliminary rulings on the cases as they come to the Court. Although these rulings are not binding on the Court judges, they inevitably provide a significant context to their work. Both the judges and the Advocates General are appointed for a six-year term that is renewable.

In tandem with the steady enlargement of EU member states and the expansion in the number of policies that is dealt with at an EU level, it is no wonder that the workload of the Court has increased significantly over the last three decades. A particular catalyst to this changed environment was the single market programme, which, unsurprisingly, brought with it an avalanche of rules and regulations on individuals, companies and member states as part of a process to achieve harmonisation in market access. A direct implication of this has been an exponential expansion of the Court's work as it both saw a dramatic growth in the number of challenges to EU law as well as being called upon to deal with matters of non-compliance. The limited resources available to the Court meant that it was even more difficult for it to deal with this increased workload. To tackle this situation a Court of First Instance was established in September 1989 with responsibility for dealing with the majority of the actions brought by individuals and companies. Since the establishment of the Court of First Instance, the Court of Justice has reverted to its traditional role of ensuring that there is a uniform interpretation of EU law, with the Court being the ultimate interpreter.

A final component in the judicial structure was the introduction in 2005 of the European Civil Service Tribunal, which was established to adjudicate on disputes between the EU and its civil service that serves the institutions of the EU (the so-called Eurocrats). Comprising seven judges, the Tribunal is attached to the Court of First Instance. The majority of the cases that have been brought to the Tribunal have been from staff employed in the European Commission, which primarily reflects the sheer number of staff employed there. Subjects have ranged from pensions to promotions and appraisals to salaries.

What, then, does the Court of Justice do? The first point to note is that the Court cannot initiate cases. Instead, it makes judgments on cases that have been referred to it from a variety of groups that range from the EU institutions, the governments of the member states, national courts, corporate bodies and individuals. In practical terms this means that the Court has the main responsibility for balancing the relative powers and influences of the EU institutions as well as the policies that have been transferred from the member states to the EU level and those that have been retained at a national level.

Although the existence of the Court of Justice is of crucial importance in establishing the presence of a European law that has primacy over national law, it is nonetheless important to stress that the Court's influence does not extend to every area of the EU. What this means in practice is that even though EU law is superior to national law, EU law has not displaced national law. A further point to note is that the reach of EU law does not extend to every area of our daily lives, as the Court of Justice can only act within the remit of the scope that has been set out in the various Treaties that govern the EU. To this end, it is apparent that the presence of the Court of Justice does not mean that there has been established a formal structure of courts that extend down from it to a local level. In this sense, the Court of Justice does not have a formal connection with the national courts in the member states, which in any case have their own cultures and traditions.

Judgments

What do a soft Greek cheese, children's building blocks and football have in common? The answer is that they have all been subject to the judgments of the European Court of Justice. On 25 October 2005 the ECJ issued a ruling that upheld the name 'feta' as a Protected Designation of Origin (PDO) for a white cheese soaked in brine that originates from Greece. The significance of this judgment was that it meant that only cheese originating from Greece could use the name 'feta' and as such offered protection to local producers from competition abroad. You may wonder why this is significant. Well, the answer can be found when we examine in closer detail the products we buy that we often think are of local origin but which upon closer inspection do not turn out to be. One of the most obvious examples of this is Cheddar cheese, which many people would consider to be quintessentially British. Yet the vast majority of Cheddar cheese consumed in Britain actually originates from countries that range from as far away as Canada to closer to home, Ireland. The reason why Cheddar is not protected in the same way is that it has been argued at a European level that the name has become too generic and as such it is used in far too many countries to allow it to be protected.

DEFENDING THE MELTON MOWBRAY PORK PIE

Whatever criticism can be levied at it for incompetence and mismanagement, the EU has nonetheless played an important role in protecting the origins of many of the foodstuffs that we love to eat which could otherwise be manufactured cheaper elsewhere. This helps to ensure that certain products, ranging from beer to cheese, that we identify with particular locations are actually made in the locations from which their reputation arises.

Within the EU there are three schemes to protect agricultural products and foodstuffs. The strictest rules apply to the Protected Designation of Origin (PDO) scheme, which officially guarantees the origin and quality of products that are produced within a specific geographical area, with products ranging from Italian Parma ham to Cornish clotted cream and Yorkshire forced rhubarb having PDO status. The second scheme relates to Protected Geographical Indication (PGI) status, which covers foodstuffs protected within a geographical area. Relevant examples include Welsh lamb and French Gruyère cheese. The third scheme is Traditional Speciality Guaranteed (TSG) status, which emphasises the traditional character of a foodstuff, such as the traditional Bramley apple pie filling.

Such is the significance of these schemes that many organisations are formed with the specific purpose of seeking PDO, PGI or TSG protection. One such association is the Melton Mowbray Pork Pie Association, which was formed in 1998 to obtain PGI status for the famous Melton Mowbray pork pie, an objective that was achieved just a decade latter when PGI status was granted on 30 June 2009. One incidental EU fact worth noting is that the chairman of the Melton Mowbray Pork Pie Association, Councillor Matthew O'Callaghan, has actually never eaten a pork pie because he is a vegetarian.

> The relevance of the Court of Justice to these schemes is that once a registration has been given to a particular product by the European Commission, it is often the case that companies challenge this decision in the Court of Justice. As such the judgments of the Court as to whether a product qualifies for such protection are of extreme importance to the local producers. From this it is clear to see how the EU can provide protection for products that would otherwise be open to competition in a globalised economy.

In another context, on 14 September 2010 the Danish company Lego lost its battle in the Court of Justice to overturn a decision taken six years earlier that cancelled Lego's trademark of its famous red toy building brick. Lego had argued that the studs on the top of its bricks were distinctive enough to enable trademark rights. However, the Court decided that this was not the case and stressed that such protection would limit the opportunities for competition. As such the decision was welcomed by Lego's main rival Mega Brands (maker of Mega Briks), which had challenged the trademark registration. An obvious consequence of this will be to open up competition.

The final example relates to the 15 December 1995 decision of the Court of Justice that the existing rules on the transfer of footballers between clubs contradicted the rights of the free movement of workers. The background to this decision was that in 1990 the relatively unknown Belgian footballer Jean-Marc Bosman wanted to move from RFC Liège to the French club Dunkirk. However, RFC Liège sought to stop this transfer by arguing that a fee had to be paid for the player in this cross-border transfer. Bosman complained against this decision and took his case to the Court of Justice where he successfully argued that the system of transfers between clubs was a restriction of services. Prior to Bosman it was only possible for a football player to move to another club when agreement was reached between both clubs. In the vast majority of cases this involved a transfer fee, which in effect meant that the buying club purchased the player from the selling club irrespective of whether the contract that a player had with the selling club had ended. Thus, a player who was out of contract was unable to sign a contract with a new team until a transfer had been paid or where the selling club had taken the decision to offer them a free transfer. There were two significant implications of this decision. First, transfer fees for out-of-contract players were illegal for players moving within the EU and therefore fees could only be paid where players still had serving contracts. Second, quota systems on foreign players were also deemed illegal, which meant that clubs within the EU could have as many players from other EU countries as they liked. This had a particularly profound effect on the game in England, where clubs that were able to benefit from lucrative media deals and brand sponsorship were suddenly able to bring a galaxy of foreign superstars into their teams.

GENDER PRICED INSURANCE

Gender has traditionally played a key role in the pricing of insurance policies.

In 2004 an EU Directive prohibited all discrimination based on sex in the access to a supply of goods or services. In principle the Directive therefore prohibited the use of gender as a method of determining insurance premiums and benefits with regard to contracts that were entered into after 21 December 2007. However, the Directive also stated differential pricing could be maintained where statistical evidence supported such an approach. Insurance companies regarded this as crucial because as women drivers are statistically proven to have fewer accidents than male drivers, premiums for female insurance policies have generally been lower. In a similar way, because women live longer, men have traditionally received a higher rate from their pension annuities because their life expectancy is lower and as such their pension savings are able to produce more income over a shorter time.

Such continued practice of price differentials was subject to a review after the Belgian Constitutional Court asked the European Court of Justice to assess the validity of differential pricing. This in turn resulted in the ECJ ruling on 1 March 2011 that insurers cannot charge different premiums to men and women based on their gender from 21 December 2012 onwards. In the case of car insurance, the significance of this ruling is that female car insurance premiums will rise while male insurance premiums will fall. And where high costs of insurance have in the past discouraged young men from buying fast cars that are more likely to lead to road accidents, a reduction in insurance costs could worryingly result in greater purchases of high performance cars.

Growth of EU law

Recent decades have seen a significant expansion in the number of cases that require decision at a European level. This is the product of the jurisdiction of the ECJ having been expanded by successive Treaty negotiations. The most recent of these, the 2009 Treaty of Lisbon, expanded the remit of the Court to cover all the activities of the EU, with the exception of the common foreign and security policy. The most recent statistics show that the number of new cases brought before the Court has increased from four in 1953 to 552 cases in 2009. Over that period, a total of 16,204 cases have been brought before the Court. In terms of the number of judgments, in 1954 the Court of Justice issued two judgments. Thirty years later in 1984 the Court issued 165 judgments, while in 2009 the Court issued 377 judgments. In total, from 1952 to 2009 the Court issued 8,267 judgments.

The vast majority of these judgments have been made since the entry into force of the Single European Act (SEA) in 1987, which vastly expanded the competences of the Community. Thus, whereas the Court of Justice made 2,292 judgments from 1952 to 1986, it made 5,975 judgments from 1987 to 2009. A discrepancy between the number of cases and judgments made is in part a cost of this increased workload, with a case often taking up to two years to be dealt with. In examining these issues in more detail, it is evident that through its case law the Court of Justice has set out the need for member states and national courts to implement EU law in full, to ensure that the rights that have been given to citizens are protected, and to correct situations where national provisions conflict with EU law. The significance of this state of affairs has over time led to a whole spectrum of society awakening to the reality of the potential benefits that can be obtained by seeking redress through the Court of Justice. As the scope of the EU's remit has expanded into such issues as the health and safety of workers, entitlements to welfare, as well as the mutual recognition of qualifications to permit the free movement of workers, it has inevitably been the case that the Court of Justice is called upon ever more frequently to make judgments on these matters. This has also extended to scenarios where there have been breaches of EU law by member states.

Challenging the member states

Somewhat inevitably the judgments that the Court has passed have often received a particularly negative reaction from the member states concerned. A classic example is the 1990 Factortame judgment, which concerned fishing rights. In this case Spanish fishermen had purchased British fishing vessels and with them the quotas that were attributable to the UK. Thus, Spanish fishermen were using British quotas to land fish that they had caught in Spain. In response to this, the British government passed the 1988 Merchant Shipping Act, which required

75% of the shareholders and directors of a company to be British so as to allow the company to be able to register itself as British. The Spanish fishermen claimed that this was a breach of their rights to be given equal status as EC citizens. Ultimately the Court ruled that the 1988 Merchant Shipping Act was a breach of EC law on the ground of equal treatment of citizens and the ruling consequently overturned the Merchant Shipping Act.

The Factortame case provides a good example of the Court overturning an Act of Parliament and thereby demonstrating the supremacy of EU law over domestic law. Commentators would therefore be correct in highlighting the fact that the case provides clear evidence of the way in which EU membership has eroded parliamentary sovereignty. At times, however, the rulings made by the ECJ can act as pivotal moments in providing outcomes that favour individuals that would otherwise not have materialised at a national level. The Court has often been the venue where the European Commission has sought redress from member states for non-compliance. At the same time, however, member states have often challenged Commission judgments in the Court. But more often than not the judicial outcome has forced member states to comply with policies from which they otherwise thought that they were exempt. And while the possibility for this scenario has existed since the foundation of the Community, the expansion of the EU's remit into policies that were once the preserve of member states has increased the potential for greater backlash at the national level against judgments that many critics perceive to erode national sovereignty.

It is plainly evident that the very existence of the European Court of Justice is often portrayed as a double-edged sword. On the one hand, its presence helps to ensure that companies, individuals and governments can be taken to account for non-compliance on European legislation, albeit with the proviso that no company, individual or member state has ever found themselves behind bars as a result of the Court's decisions. At the same time, the Court does provide an opportunity for appeal and judicial redress. Yet many people would be correct in their analysis if they considered that the Court had gone further than the expectations initially set out by the founding fathers.

For what it is worth, the Court itself faces a classic dilemma because if it takes a judgment that confirms and supports a European policy then it is inevitably going to be accused of being pro-integrationist, and if it does not then it will be regarded as being a sop to the member state governments. However, on balance it is true that the Court has favoured many solutions that have been of a pro-integrationist nature and as such has been at the forefront of the EU institutions that have played a leading role in deepening integration. This has not only been emphasised by landmark judgments, but more fundamentally its significance has been shown through the number of cases it has considered, although one inevitable consequence of this has been a diminution in the efficiency of the Court because of the length of time it can take for judgments to be dealt with.

9
The European single currency

Of all the policies that have emerged in the history of European integration, the European single currency has been subject to the greatest degree of debate. This is not surprising given that a national currency is one of the most identifiable features of a nation state. Any initiative that seeks to replace a national currency is going to provoke a great deal of discussion about the positive and negative aspects of such a strategy. A key motivation behind the launch of the European single currency – the 'euro' – in 1999 was the belief that it would improve the economic fortunes of the EU. This was because there was a view that the benefits of the single market, which allowed the free movement of people, goods, services and capital, would always be limited through the presence of individual national currencies. But while the arguments behind the creation of the euro had strong economic considerations, it was also evident that such a process had considerable political implications. It not only brought the participating member states closer together, but was regarded as a means of deepening European integration.

Background

The origins of the euro can be traced back to 1969 when in February of that year the Barre Report advocated that the economic policies of the then six member states should be co-ordinated with a view to achieving closer monetary co-operation. A few months later agreement was reached at the December 1969 Hague Summit that Economic and Monetary Union (EMU) was to be an official goal of European integration. To investigate what would be required for such an objective to be achieved, the Hague meeting agreed to a major study on EMU to be conducted under the chairmanship of the then Luxembourg Prime Minister, Pierre Werner. When this study was completed in October 1970, the Werner Report set out a path for the achievement of monetary union by 1980. This was a very ambitious goal, given that the Community had only just created a Customs Union in 1968. A combination of the ambi-tious nature of the proposal and the economic difficulties that dogged the 1970s meant that it was impossible to make any progress towards monetary union as member states were preoc-cupied with dealing with the impact of oil price rises and high levels of unemployment.

By the end of the 1970s discussion was once again taking place about the possibility of monetary union. The chief driving force behind this initiative was the President of the European Commission, Roy Jenkins, who was keen that the Community should reclaim the goal of monetary union. As in the Werner Report, it was Jenkins's belief that by bringing the economic policies of the member states together there would be a consid-erable benefit to economic growth. This led to the establishment of the European Monetary System (EMS) in 1979, which was created to provide greater economic co-ordination between the member states. To achieve this aim, a European Currency Unit (ECU) was created that could act as a parallel currency while an Exchange Rate Mechanism (ERM) was established to reduce exchange rate instability by fixing the exchange rates of the par-ticipating currencies. The idea behind the ERM was that reduc-tions in the fluctuation in exchange rate currencies would provide a stronger environment for economic growth. This was because there would be more stable prices in relation to the import and export of goods within the Community as well as between the Community and non-member states.

For much of the 1980s this system had considerable success in reducing exchange rate fluctuation, which in turn assisted with reductions in member states' inflation rates. This therefore created a more positive economic environment. The success of the ERM in providing a framework for monetary stability created a belief among some member states and the European Commission that it could be possible to achieve monetary union as a means of completing the single market. In their view, different national currencies were a hindrance to business competitiveness, not least because of the transaction costs associated with exchanging one currency for another.

Apart from the desire to eliminate unnecessary transaction costs, the business community was additionally arguing that volatility in exchange rates impacted on competitiveness. This was because currency fluctuation resulted in price variations for products imported from and exported to other member states. Many businesses were also keen on the idea of a single currency because they thought that it would allow them to standardise certain procedures across the member states that adopted a single currency, such as purchasing and payroll. In addition to these points of view, some EU member states argued that a single currency would help to enhance the influence of the EU at the global level by creating a new currency to challenge the US dollar and Japanese yen.

The argument that a single currency was a necessary element to the completion of the single market was not shared by all member states or business groups. Britain was in the vanguard of those states that were unwilling to give up national sovereignty on monetary policy. This was despite the fact that there was a recognition that some economic benefits could accrue from such a move.

The President of the European Commission, Jacques Delors, was a particularly influential figure in these debates. In June 1988 Delors was asked by the leaders of the EU member states to chair a committee to examine the possibility of creating a single currency. The work of the committee was completed in April 1989, with the Delors Report setting out a three-stage approach to creating monetary union. The member states accepted the report at the June 1989 Madrid European Council. This in turn led the member states to agree at the December 1989 Strasbourg European Council that an intergovernmental conference (IGC) had to be established so as to set out in detail what would be required to move towards monetary union.

In the course of 1990 the economic arguments in favour of monetary union became conflated with political considerations that arose out of the collapse of Communism in Central and Eastern Europe. A key issue for the Community was not just how it would respond to these events, but more specifically the implications of German reunification in October 1990. Although reunification meant that Germany became the largest member state, since the 1970s West Germany had been the driving economic force of the Community. This meant that the West German currency, the Deutschmark, had been the dominant currency. As a result, the West German central bank, the Bundesbank, was of far greater importance in the European currency arena than the central banks of other member states that were in this sense tied to a de facto Deutschmark zone.

For the French President François Mitterrand, a key motivation in establishing a European single currency and therefore a European Central Bank was that it would counter the power of the Bundesbank. In Mitterrand's eyes this would consequently tie Germany down 'Gulliver-like'. For other countries, such as Greece, Italy, Portugal and Spain, a single European currency held out the opportunity of replacing somewhat weaker currencies. Such Machiavellian objectives were largely ignored by Germany.

It too was attracted to a single currency, albeit for different reasons.

For Germany, the objective of a single currency rested in the legacy of the Second World War and the concerns that still existed at that time among its own population as well as the populations of other member states that there was a need to cement Germany's position firmly within Europe. German Chancellor Helmut Kohl considered that the best means of assuaging concern among his own people as well as the populations of other member states about the rebirth of Germany was to replace the Deutschmark with a new single currency that all participating member states would be able to influence. But this of course was potentially a huge risk for Germany. The Bundesbank had developed the Deutschmark into Europe's leading currency, with it being a sign of Germany's economic revival after 1945. As Jacques Delors would later comment in the *Financial Times* on 15 December 1998, 'Not all Germans believe in God but they all believe in the Bundesbank.'

Creating a single currency

But how would a single currency operate? How could the economies of the member states converge so that they were economically fit enough to participate in a single currency? After all, a single currency would have a single central bank that would control inflation across all participating states through a single interest rate. Could it be that Spain's economic concerns would be the same as Germany's, or Italy's the same as Belgium's? Since the start of discussions about a single currency the best and the brightest of Europe's (and the world's) economists and political scientists have been found mulling over these sorts of issues. Some have come to the conclusion that a single currency just could not work. This has included many pro-Europeans who have argued 'yes to Europe, but no to the single currency'. For them the complexity of tying the likes of Greece, Ireland, Portugal and Spain – with their weaker economies – into a system with stronger economies such as France and Germany was an impossible task. This was because the economic differences between the participating countries would be too great for a single currency to operate in a stable and effective manner.

Given these concerns, as well as Germany's own insistence that any replacement for the Deutschmark had to be economically stable, a central concern of the IGC negotiations on monetary union was to design a strong and stable single currency. These negotiations were concluded at the December 1991 Maastricht European Council, when member states reached agreement on a Treaty on European Union, otherwise known as the Maastricht Treaty. The Treaty established a three-stage route to monetary union, noting that a monetary union would be established by 1999 at the latest.

Maastricht Approach to Monetary Union

First stage	1 July 1990–31 December 2003	• Free movement of capital between member states. • Co-operation between central banks. • Closer co-operation between member states economic policies.
Second stage	1 January 1994– 31 December 1998	• Convergence of the member states' economic and monetary policies.
Third stage	From 1 January 1999	• Creation of a European Central Bank. • Fixing of exchange rates. • Introduction of a single currency.

For a member state to proceed to monetary union it had to meet a specific set of convergence criteria:

- a maximum annual budget deficit of not more than 3% of gross domestic product (GDP);
- a total public sector debt not exceeding 60% of GDP;
- a rate of inflation not exceeding 1.5% above the three lowest inflation countries within the EU;
- a long-term interest rate to be no more than 2% higher than that of the three best performers;
- and for there to have been no realignments within the ERM.

The creation of a monetary union also necessitated the building of institutions to govern the single currency. A European Central Bank was established that would be responsible for issuing euro notes and coins as well as deciding on the common interest rate that would be applied to all members of the single currency. The European Commission was given the responsibility to monitor the financial stability of the member states participating in the single currency as well as to make judgments on the extent to which member states were ready to join. But while such institutions were necessary to run the single currency, little thought was given to the deeper structural implications of the single currency being the first monetary union without fiscal union. What this meant was that whereas the single currency provided for the management of monetary policy through a European Central Bank, member states retained control over fiscal policy, namely government expenditure and taxation. For many observers this was an intrinsic weakness of the single currency, as participating member states would not be required to implement the same fiscal policies, thereby creating euro instability.

While all member states signed the Maastricht Treaty, agreement was only possible with the provision that Britain would not be committed to joining a single currency. This opt-out was extended to Denmark in December 1992 so as to placate the Danish electorate who rejected the Maastricht Treaty in a referendum vote in June of that year. Above all, Britain and Denmark's opposition to the single currency was grounded in their view that it would limit their ability to exercise freedom over economic policy as, among other factors, a single currency would require a common interest rate for all members. As such, interest rates could not be varied according to particular national concerns.

For the British public, their government's reluctance to join the single currency was confounded on 16 September 1992 when Britain was forced out of the ERM as a result of intense speculation against the pound. The following day, the Italian lira was forced to leave the system. In both cases, currency speculators believed that the currencies were overvalued and that there was a need for them to be depreciated. The pound and lira's exit from the ERM raised a question mark over the stability of the monetary union project. This was confirmed by continued instability in the remaining ERM currencies throughout the remainder of 1992 and until the late summer of 1993. In August 1993 the ERM came under such intense pressure that the remaining currencies were allowed 15% fluctuation margins either side of the value that they were set within the system.

Analysis of these events pointed to the conclusion that EU member states were not ready to progress to a single currency. Yet, in contrast to this interpretation, others suggested that only through the establishment of a single currency could the currency speculators be defeated. It was certainly the case that French President François Mitterrand and German Chancellor Helmut Kohl were resolute in their support for monetary union. A concern that monetary union could not be delayed or pushed off track had resulted in their insistence on a clear timetable in the Maastricht Treaty for the establishment of a single currency.

Finally a concern about the importance of ensuring the stability of countries joining the single currency meant that member states reached agreement at the Dublin European Council of December 1996 on a stability and growth pact to ensure that those member states that participated in the single currency would not undermine the stability of the euro economy. In particular, while governments would be able to pursue their own independent fiscal policy, they would only be allowed to borrow to a maximum of 3% of their annual GDP and had to ensure that all public debt would not be in excess of 60% of GDP. It was also agreed that the Commission had the powers to fine any member state that breached the terms of the pact.

The Road to the Single Currency

1969	Hague Summit sets goal of EMU by 1980.
1970	Werner Report provided the first plans for economic and monetary union.
1979	European Monetary System (EMS) starts working.
1989	Delors Report on EMU was published.
1990	Stage I of EMU formally began.
1991	Agreement at Maastricht European Council on a Treaty on European Union, incorporating EMU.
1992	ERM crisis.
1994	Stage II of EMU formally began. The European Monetary Institute was established in Frankfurt as a precursor to a European Central Bank.
1999	Establishment of the single currency.
2002	Introduction of euro banknotes and coins and withdrawal of national banknotes and coins.

Getting economically fit to join

A direct implication of the convergence criteria and the terms of the stability pact was that many of the governments who wished to participate in the single currency had to limit public sector spending so as to reduce the amount of government debt. Yet such rules were particularly problematic for member state governments, which had to grapple with a period of economic slowdown from the late 1990s onwards. Faced with the combination of declining economic growth, rising unemployment, increased expenditure and lower taxation, it was inevitable that many governments found it difficult to stay within the 3% budget deficit limit. France and Germany broke the 3% limit in 2002 and 2003. The view that if the strongest economies in Europe found it hard to stay within such limits then the weaker economies would find it impossible led the President of the Commission, Romano Prodi, to refer to the stability pact as 'stupid' in 2002. This would in turn result in the terms of the stability pact being relaxed in March 2005 so that a member state could exceed the 3% limit if it was undertaking expenditure policies that were in parallel with 'European goals' and 'fostering international solidarity'. Such broad goals therefore allowed governments a degree of flexibility over how they conducted their economic policy. While this flexibility was viewed as a positive development, it provided further evidence of the complexity of marshalling a group of countries with different economic conditions towards a single currency.

Although the economic difficulties that beset European countries in the early years of the twenty-first century were a cause for concern, a number of European governments had broader structural economic problems that raised questions about the extent to which they were fit to participate in a single currency. For instance, public debt levels often exceeded the

60% ceiling. Public debt in Belgium and Italy was near double this amount. In addition to these difficulties, there was also notable divergence in the way that the economies of the different member states were run. Some, such as Britain and Germany, had a stronger climate of free competition. Yet for others, such as Greece and Italy, economic competition was far less dynamic, with many jobs and contracts being dependent on personal contacts. These economies also suffered from a higher percentage of illegal economic activity. In Southern Italy this 'black economy' has traditionally accounted for nearly one-quarter of its GDP and as a result the Italian economy as a whole has suffered from lower tax revenues, with business competitiveness adversely affected by organised crime.

The reality of this state of affairs meant that there were serious concerns about whether the economic benefits for business of a single currency could paper over its design weaknesses. One of the key problems was that member states still retained control over their own national budgets. As a result a member of the single currency could potentially undertake policies at a national level that might destabilise the broader currency zone. The structural differences between member states were highlighted by the fact that the Italian government had a special one-off 'euro tax' to boost its revenues so as to meet the terms of participating in the single currency.

In the end, when it came to taking a decision on which countries should participate in the single currency, the political driving force was given greater prominence than the underlying economic differentials between the member states. This meant that when the single currency was finally established in 1999, Greece was the only country that was deemed not to have met the terms of the convergence criteria out of those countries that wished to join. Thus, on 1 January 1999 Austria, Belgium, Finland, France, Germany, Ireland, Italy, Luxembourg, the Netherlands, Portugal and Spain established the eurozone. After having been deemed to have made improvements in its economic fortunes, Greece joined the eurozone in 2001.

Between 1999 and 2002 the euro was used as an electronic currency for foreign exchange transactions. Euro banknotes and coins were introduced on 1 January 2002 and by the end of February 2002 each of the national currencies of the twelve eurozone member states passed into history. From German Deutschmarks to Austrian schillings, all became collectors' items. A condition of those countries that joined the EU from then onwards was that they would join the eurozone if they met the necessary economic criteria. In due course, Slovenia (2007), Cyprus and Malta (2008), Slovakia (2009) and Estonia (2011) adopted the euro. By 2012 seventeen of the twenty-seven member states had adopted the euro. The remainder, with the exception of Britain and Denmark, have yet to meet the conditions for adopting the single currency. Those EU member states outside the single currency have been conscious of the impact that non-participation has in terms of reducing their economic and political influence within the EU. This came to the fore in 1998 with the formation of the Eurogroup consisting of the eurozone Finance Ministers. Moreover, EU member states that are outside the euro are nonetheless influenced by euro policies that they have little influence over as their currencies are pegged to the euro. Finally outside the EU the euro has been used as the national currency of Kosovo and Montenegro as well as in a number of micro states such as Andorra, Monaco, San Marino and the Vatican City.

Implications

Creating a single currency does, of course, have implications for national monetary sovereignty. In most countries the national currency is one of the key symbols of national identity.

The United States of America is synonymous with the dollar, Russia with the rouble, Japan with the yen, China with the yuan renminbi. The same could be said for many European countries. France with the franc, Germany with the Deutschmark, Italy with the lira. But while many observers may comment that the single currency has impacted on national identity, France, say, does not appear to be any less French for its participation in the single currency.

THE EURO AS AN INTERNATIONAL CURRENCY

A notable argument in favour of the single currency was that it would provide the EU with a currency that had a global reach and as such could be viewed in parallel with the US dollar and Japanese yen as an international currency. The evidence of the early years of the euro was that the combination of the weight of the euro area in the world economy and an increasing use of the euro as a means of financial transactions resulted in the euro quickly emerging as the second most traded currency after the US dollar. Many governments inside and outside the EU also started to accumulate significant holdings of euros as part of their foreign exchange reserves. The rising popularity of the euro led some governments to replace gold reserves with euros. But while this decision was viewed in the early years of this century as a wise move because of the declining value of gold, the subsequent turmoil in the international economy resulted in the value of gold appreciating, because at a time of uncertainty investors turn to reliable assets such as gold. In the case of Britain, the decision of the Labour government to sell four hundred tons of gold between 1999 and 2002 to be replaced by euros meant that a subsequent depreciation in the value of euros and a near quadrupling in the price of gold had cost taxpayers almost £7 billion by 2010.

Governments participating in the single currency are no longer able to exercise full control over their economic policy. At first glance this is often equated to their ability to increase or decrease interest rates, as a single currency requires a common interest rate controlled by a European Central Bank. Interest rates cannot be varied according to particular national concern. This loss of control also extends to the fact that membership of the single currency requires governments to adhere to strict economic criteria, such as maintaining low budget deficits. In addition to these concerns over the conduct of macroeconomic policy, opponents of monetary integration equally point to the conversion costs associated with participation in the single currency, such as the reprogramming of shop tills.

Set against these points, advocates of the single currency tend to put the concern about a loss of sovereignty within a wider context, whereby the forces of globalisation mean that national economic policy is affected by a variety of factors that a government is essentially powerless to control. For some countries, such as Greece and Italy, the benefit of a single currency was regarded as outweighing any economic costs. This was because their governments had traditionally been less successful in delivering such objectives as a stable economy and low inflation. In particular, the weaker economies of the EU that joined the euro suddenly found themselves going from a poor to a good credit rating. This was essentially because, with the introduction of the euro, the money markets concluded that if the poorer members of the euro were ever to find themselves in difficulty then the richer euro countries would come to their assistance. What this meant in practice was that the weaker economies were able to borrow money at cheaper rates of interest than had traditionally been the case. As a result both consumers and governments in Greece, Ireland, Portugal, Spain and many other eurozone countries went on a massive credit binge, which resulted in the amounting of massive debts. In Greece this materialised in an expansion in the size of the public sector and a near doubling of public sector wages in the period since the introduction of the euro. This contributed to Greece having in 2011 a public debt in excess of €340 billion for a country of only 11 million people. The problematic nature of these debt levels was compounded by Greece experiencing a decline in tourism export revenues and a system of weak tax collection, which meant that the Greek government did not receive sufficient income to cover its debts.

In the early years of the euro the implications of rising debt levels was largely overlooked by governments and businesses, which viewed a single currency in positive terms. A key factor here was that the elimination of national currencies (and the transaction costs involved) made it easier to conduct business, while high debt levels were offset by low interest rates, which made the cost of borrowing manageable. For many businesses the euro also assisted with the export of products. This was because the value of the euro reflected the sum of all the eurozone economies, which meant that for German businesses the euro became a weaker currency than would have been the case if the Deutschmark had continued to exist. As a result the price of German goods became cheaper for export after the euro was introduced, leading to significant growth in the volume of German exports. And the fact that such export growth continued after the financial crisis – with German exports increasing by 18% between August 2009 and May 2011 – was due to low eurozone interest rates.

SOVEREIGN DEBT

Governments have two main ways in which they can raise money to fund expenditure. The first is taxation. The second is by raising money from investors to buy its bonds, which the government then guarantees to repay at a future time. Investors are often happy to lend money to governments because bonds are recognised as a safe investment. This is because governments can raise taxes to repay the debt. Risk does, however, vary according to the country concerned. In the 1980s many Latin American countries defaulted on repaying their bonds, as did Russia and Turkey in the 1990s. The extent to which a government is likely to default on a bond is reflected in its credit scoring by agencies such as Standard and Poor, Moody's and Fitch Ratings. AAA is the best rating. DDD is the worst. A lower rating means that a government has to offer a greater return to investors by offering higher interest rates. This in turn means that the cost of government borrowing increases. Since the 1990s there has been an explosion in the levels of European private and government debt.

The financial crisis of 2008 witnessed a ballooning of government debt as governments had to borrow money to bail out the banking sector. By November 2011 Italy was Europe's largest bond issuer with outstanding government debt of €1.9 trillion, or 120% of its GDP. This accounted for 25% of all debt in the eurozone. Such high levels of debt have created fears in the bond markets as investors worry about the ability of governments to pay back their borrowing. This in turn means that the cost of borrowing for such governments increases as investors require greater returns to offset risks. For Italy this meant that in November 2011 the cost of an Italian ten year bond rose above 7% for the first time since it joined the euro. The significance of this is that bond yields in excess of 5% are regarded as being unsustainable.

Concerns such as these can result in a downgrading of a country's credit rating. In January 2009 Ireland was the first EU country to have its AAA credit rating given a negative outlook by Moody's. By November 2011 Greece, Portugal, and Spain all had their credit ratings reduced. This consequently increased the cost of borrowing by the Irish government as investors demanded higher interest rates for their funds. But investors also require governments to reduce their budget deficits by tightening government expenditure. Cuts to public expenditure programmes are therefore determined by investor confidence rather than political ideology. And while it may be tempting for governments to default on their loans by not paying them back and/or to let inflation rise (thereby reducing the overall value of the debt), such actions can reduce the willingness of investors to lend money in the future. The ultimate lesson is that we have to live within our means.

Economic crisis

Although the economic crisis that gripped much of the industrialised world in 2008 focused on the implications of the bad lending decisions of banks, in 2009 this crisis turned its focus to the eurozone. This was because a newly elected Greek government admitted in December 2009 that it had a total public sector debt of 113% of its GDP, which was near double the eurozone limit of 60%. The following month the Greek government announced that its annual budget deficit for 2009 had to be revised upwards from 3.7% of GDP to 12.7%. This was in turn revised to 13.6% of GDP in April 2010. The perilous state of Greece's finances raised concerns about its ability to repay its debts through generating revenue. This resulted in the cost of Greek government borrowing increasing as investors began to require higher interest rates from the loans they supplied. Investor concern quickly spread to other eurozone countries that were well known to have high levels of debt. Ireland, Italy, Portugal and Spain soon found themselves under attack.

In response to this situation, EU leaders agreed a €22 billion safety net to help Greece in February 2010. This was followed by €30 billion of emergency loans two months later in April, and was itself followed by a €110 multi-billion loan in May 2010. However, this bailout failed to quell investor anxiety about the state of the eurozone, particularly the peripheral member states of Greece, Ireland, Portugal and Spain. Ireland received a €85 billion rescue package in November 2010; Portugal was given €78 billion in May 2011. A further bailout of €109 billion was applied to Greece in July 2011, and when this was not considered enough an EU summit was held in October 2011 with the purpose of solving the crisis once and for all. The summit was considered necessary because, while the initial bailout to Greece had been regarded as sufficient to contain the economic crisis, the subsequent bailouts to Ireland and Portugal (along with the second bailout to Greece) demonstrated the inadequacy of Europe's plans. Thus, in an effort to get to grips with the situation, Europe's leaders agreed to increase the size of the European Financial Stability Mechanism to €1 trillion and for banks to write off 50% of Greek debt and provide it with an additional bailout of €130 billion.

This deal was quickly thrown in doubt when the Greek Prime Minister, George Papandreou, surprised EU leaders and his own government by announcing a referendum vote on it. Faced with this threat of brinkmanship, the other eurozone governments threatened to cut off an overdue tranche of €8 billion in aid to Greece to exert pressure on Athens to reverse the refinancing plans. A combination of concern that cutting off the aid would have prevented the Greek government from paying hundreds of thousands of public sector employees and a lack of consensus among the Greek government about the Prime Minister's initiative resulted in the referendum plan being dropped. This in turn brought about the resignation of Prime Minister Papandreou, to be replaced by a technocratic government headed by the former Governor of the Bank of Greece, Lucas Papademos. The significance of the appointment of the unelected Papademos was that it resulted in considerable concern that the EU-driven austerity measures were subverting the population's right to democratic rule.

REFERENDUM DIFFICULTIES

While Greek Prime Minister George Papandreou made a commitment to hold a referendum on the austerity plan to tackle the financial crisis, it drastically backfired and brought about his resignation. Commitments to hold referendums are used by governments as a means of gaining the support of the electorate for complex or difficult issues. In the history of the EU, referendums have often been used when countries join: Denmark (1972); Finland, Sweden and Austria (1994); and the Czech Republic, Latvia, Lithuania, Malta, Poland, Slovakia, Slovenia and Hungary (2003). But this desire to engage in such 'direct democracy' comes with the risk of proposals being rejected. Norway's application to join the EU was rejected in referendum votes in 1972 and 1994. EU Treaties have also often been subject to referendum vote, sometimes resulting in rejection. This was notably the case with the Constitutional Treaty in 2005. And while one view might be that governments should only hold referendums if they know what the answer will be, referendums tend to produce populist results that are not always concerned with the issue in question. In this sense they are more often than not a vote about the popularity of the government of the day.

Greece lightning

The Greek drama demonstrated the pivotal position that some countries occupy within the EU and particularly within the eurozone. Greece faced a particular difficulty because it did not have sufficient financial reserves to pay its loans and was moreover unable to raise additional funds from taxing a population that faced severe economic austerity measures. Faced with this situation, eurozone leaders had to write off 50% of Greek debts to lessen the debt burden on the country. Despite the significance of these events, the real concern was the economic situation in Italy rather than Greece. This was the product of two factors. The first was that the size of the Italian debt was greater than that of Greece, Ireland, Portugal and Spain combined. Standing at €1.9 trillion, the EU could not bail out Italy in the same way that it had with other countries. Secondly, investors were concerned that the Italian Prime Minister, Silvio Berlusconi, was politically unable to lead the structural reforms that were necessary to improve Italy's economic performance. The intensity of these pressures resulted in the subsequent resignation of Berlusconi in November 2011 and his replacement by the former Italian EU Commissioner, Mario Monti. As with Greece, Monti was appointed to head a technocratic government made up of experts rather than elected politicians.

Taken as a whole, these events demonstrate the implications of excessive government borrowing and the need for countries to have credible political leadership. The events also raise questions as to the appropriateness of the 'one-size-fits-all' nature of the eurozone and whether it is possible to establish a single monetary and fiscal policy that best represents the interests of all those participating in it. The eurozone crisis has brought to the fore a debate about the nature of the social contract that since the 1980s has been viewed as a central pillar of the European project. This has resulted in generous pay and munificent benefits such as lengthy holidays. But these benefits need to be paid for. When combined with what can often be excessive regulation in some member states (such as Spain), it resulted in the calamitous situation of excessive budget deficits being required to finance state benefits at a time of low competitiveness. The remedy for this state of affairs is not just the provision of funds to bail out budget deficits, but rather the need for economic and political restructuring.

A final point to note is that although their technocratic governments were brought about by Greece and Italy's massive borrowing, they are not a new development in the EU. Greece had a technocratic government in 1989–90 and Italy had a number of such governments in the 1990s. But the creation of these technocratic governments is nonetheless a significant development. Not only do they raise concerns about the rise of unelected governments, but they also highlight the failure of elected governments to deal with financial problems. It is also the case that any criticism of the technocratic governments needs to be put in the context that parliaments continue to operate in Greece and Italy and democracy therefore continues. Finally many governments around the world also include professionals who can be regarded as technocrats, of which the US is an obvious example.

The Eurozone Crisis	
December 2008	EU leaders agree on a €200 billion stimulus package to assist with economic growth.
April 2009	EU instructs France, Greece, Ireland and Spain to reduce budget deficits.
December 2009	Newly elected Greek government led by George Papandreou admits that government debts had reached €300 billion, equivalent to 113% of its GDP. This is nearly double the eurozone limit of 60%. In response, ratings agencies start downgrading Greek bank and government debt because of a concern that Greece will default on its debts.
January 2010	EU auditors find that Greece has accounting irregularities. As a result the Greek budget deficit for 2009 is revised upwards from 3.7% of GDP to 12.7%, more than four times EU rules. ·
February 2010	Concern about Greek economic fortunes spreads to other EU countries, notably Ireland, Portugal and Spain. Greek government implements austerity measures.
March 2010	The eurozone countries and the International Monetary Fund (IMF) establish a €22 billion safety net to help Greece.
April 2010	Eurozone countries provide €30 billion of emergency loans to Greece. Greek budget deficit is revealed to be 13.6% of GDP and not 12.7%.

May 2010 | The eurozone and the IMF agree on a €110 billion bailout package to assist Greece.

November 2010 | Continuing instability in the eurozone results in Ireland receiving a €85 billion rescue package from the eurozone and the IMF.

February 2011 | Eurozone Finance Ministers establish a bailout fund called the European Financial Stability Mechanism backed by €500 billion.

May 2011 | Portugal receives a €78 billion bailout from the eurozone and the IMF.

June 2011 | Greece is told by eurozone government ministers to implement severe austerity measures, otherwise the country will default on the payment of its debts.

July 2011 | EU provides a further bailout fund of €109 billion to resolve the Greek debt crisis and stop the financial difficulties spreading to other EU economies. The three main credit rating agencies – Standard and Poor, Moody's and Fitch Ratings – lower Greece's credit rating to a level that is associated with there being a high likelihood of it defaulting on its loans.

October 2011 | At a crucial summit on the euro crisis, eurozone leaders agree to increase the size of the European Financial Stability Mechanism to €1 trillion, to write off 50% of Greek debt and to provide the Greek government with €130 billion.

December 2011 | In an effort to tackle the crisis, France and Germany hope that EU leaders can agree on Treaty change to support the euro. Britain's refusal to sign up to Treaty change means that the agreement on a separate eurozone pact to establish stronger economic discipline cannot be enforced EU wide.

The end of the euro?

In reviewing the financial crisis, it is evident that at its heart sits the problem of having a single currency without fiscal union, and the difficulty of bringing together the wealthy Northern European economies with the poorer economies of Southern Europe. At the time of the negotiation of the Maastricht Treaty, a combination of these concerns and a distaste for the encroachment of the EU onto domestic monetary sovereignty resulted in the British government negotiating an opt-out from the single currency. This was a position that would be later followed by Denmark. In taking such a position both countries were viewed as being awkward partners. Yet the financial crisis that has played out across the EU has highlighted that with hindsight there was much sense in Britain's arguments. This should not result in great glee on the streets of London and Copenhagen. In the case of Britain, two-thirds of its exports are to the eurozone and Britain's economic health is critically linked to that of the eurozone. The eurozone crisis is the most significant that Europe has faced since the Second World War and the ramifications of a collapse in the euro are unthinkable.

To remedy matters it is evident that there is a need for the eurozone to tackle the issue of having a single currency without fiscal union. In other words, the European Central Bank, which controls the euro and has responsibility for setting interest rates, does not have control over national monetary policy, such as spending decisions and interest rates. This has allowed eurozone governments to pursue destabilising economic policies. The antidote of fiscal union is a political solution that will require eurozone countries to give up their budgetary sovereignty. Instead, their economies will be subject to direct supervision by the likes of a super-Finance Minister who will be able to demand that national budgets be changed if they undermine the eurozone.

The solution of fiscal union is not without its consequences. Fiscal union will create a far more integrated eurozone and will further clarify the distinction between members and non-members, with the latter being excluded from what will be a core aspect of EU decision making. Non-eurozone member states will inevitably raise concerns about the wider nature of their country's relationship with the EU, with the possibility of them seeking to repatriate aspects of policy that they are no longer able to influence.

10

The EU and the world

From the end of the Second World War until the collapse of the
Berlin Wall in 1989, world politics was dominated by the superpower struggle between the United States and the Soviet Union.
During this period the EU's engagement in external policies was
primarily related to trade and development co-operation. But
with the collapse of the Berlin Wall and the subsequent implo-
sion of the Soviet Union in 1991, EU member states set about
establishing a stronger collective foreign policy. This included
developing stronger relations with its near neighbours in Central
and Eastern Europe, leading to the enlargement of the EU.
A stronger EU foreign policy necessitated the development of
the structures for the EU to act more cohesively and confidently
on foreign policy matters, which in turn necessitated a military
dimension. The perceived need to develop the EU's foreign,
security and defence capacities resulted in tension between the
willingness of member states to work collectively and their desire
to retain independent national positions. This quickly resulted in
the conclusion that there was a 'capability–expectations gap' with
regard to the EU's ability to be an effective actor in the international arena. Some twenty years later it is evident that the rhet-
oric that has often been attached to establishing a stronger EU
role in external affairs has not always been matched by the necessary commitment, structures and policies to ensure the provision
of effective policies.

Size matters

A combination of EU enlargement and expansion in the number of policies that are dealt with at a European level has meant that the EU plays an important global role. In 2012 the twenty-seven member states had a total population of 502 million. At the same time the population of China was 1.34 billion, India 1.22 billion and the United States 310 million. If the populations of EU member states were to be counted on an individual basis, none would be listed in the ten most populous countries in the world. Such statistics are particularly noteworthy because they empha-sise that in negotiations with key economic powerhouses such as China, the USA, India, Brazil and Russia, the combined popula-tion of the EU helps to ensure it is able to deliver benefits that would otherwise be harder to obtain. The EU's global influence is, however, not just dependent on population size.

Estimated Population of the Ten Largest Countries in the World in 2012	
1. China	1.34 billion
2. India	1.22 billion
European Union	**502 million**
3. United States	310 million
4. Indonesia	239 million
5. Brazil	193 million
6. Pakistan	173 million
7. Nigeria	158 million
8. Bangladesh	142 million
9. Russia	142 million
10. Japan	127 million

The most recent accurate information shows that when we rank countries according to Gross Domestic Product (GDP), we find that four of the EU member states are in the world's richest ten countries. And while this position will inevitably decline as other countries in the world develop their economies, it is nonetheless the case that by 2020 it is predicted that three of the world's top ten countries by GDP will still come from the EU. Thus, despite the eurozone crisis highlighting the economic difficulties that many EU countries face – as well as emphasising a shift of global influence towards the East – the highly developed nature of EU economies means that they will continue to be an important influence globally in the years ahead. This is because EU economies consume vast amounts of goods imported from developing countries and at the same time are significant exporters of technology and products such as financial services and luxury brands that are increasingly in demand by the expanding middle classes of developing countries. In this ever more interconnected world it is evident that the growing economic and political pressures from Brazil, Russia, India and China means that the collective influence of the EU as a whole is crucially important in securing outcomes that benefit the EU member states.

World's Ten Richest Countries as Defined by GDP in 2010 and 2020 (US $ Billions)

Ranking	Country	GDP 2010 (US $ million)	Country	GDP 2020 (US $ million)
1	USA	14,802,001	China	28,124,070
2	China	9,711,244	USA	22,644,910
3	Japan	4,267,942	India	10,255,943
4	India	3,912,991	Japan	6,196,979
5	Germany	2,861,117	Russia	4,326,987
6	Russia	2,211,755	Germany	3,981,033

Cont'd

Ranking	Country	GDP 2010 (US $ million)	Country	GDP 2020 (US $ million)
7	United Kingdom	2,183,277	Brazil	3,868,813
8	France	2,154,399	United Kingdom	3,360,442
9	Brazil	2,154,399	France	3,214,921
10	Italy	1,767,120	Mexico	2,838,722

Source: Euromonitor

Trade policy

The EU's ability to exercise influence at a world level has traditionally been most evident in the area of trade policy. One of the most important arguments outlined by the founding fathers of European integration was that the removal of tariff barriers between countries helped to integrate countries and establish peace and security. From humble beginnings, trade between the EU member states has expanded greatly to the extent that the most recent statistics published in 2011 demonstrate that the EU accounts for the largest percentage of imports and exports of world goods and services.

World Trade in Goods and Services, 2011

Country	Imports (€ billions)	Exports (€ billions)
EU 27	17.5%	16.9%
USA	15.7%	12.2%
China	10.7%	11.9%

Cont'd

Country	Imports (€ billions)	Exports (€ billions)
Association of South-East Asian Nations (ASEAN)	8.0%	8.7%
Latin America	6.8%	6.6%
Japan	5.7%	6.2%
South Korea	3.5%	3.7%
Canada	3.3%	3.1%
European Free Trade Association (EFTA; Iceland, Norway, Liechtenstein, Switzerland)	2.3%	3.1%
Russia	2.2%	3.0%
Candidates	1.6%	1.2%
Other	22.7%	23.3%

Source: European Union in the World, 2011.

The Treaty of Rome initially established a Common Commercial Policy (CCP) by which the then Community managed the agreements (and disputes) that emerged out of the commitment to have a Customs Union. The Customs Union required the member states to establish a common external trade tariff, which meant that there was just one trade policy instead of having different national trade policies. Thus, goods entering the EU would be subject to the same customs duty. The CCP was more than just about setting a rate of duty. It necessitated the establishment of agreements with non-EU member states (otherwise known as 'third countries') that sought to open up EU markets to these countries and at the same time allow companies in EU member states to gain access to the markets of the third countries.

To achieve these outcomes it was agreed that the European Commission would be entrusted with negotiating on behalf of the member states. In this sense, trade is a good example of a policy area where the member states have relinquished national sovereignty to the EU level. That is not to say that the member states have become supine to the Commission's influence. Rather, while the Commission has the authority to negotiate on behalf of the EU, it does so on a mandate provided by the member states via the Council of Ministers. What this means is that trade nego- tiations bring together many different interests from within the EU as well as external countries. In undertaking these tasks the Commission has established a whole series of trade agreements that cover every corner of the world. And while many of these agreements are of a bilateral nature between the EU and a specific country, such as China, many more are with regional groupings such as the Association of South-East Asian Nations (ASEAN). Others are of a multilateral nature, such as the World Trade Organisation (WTO), which has 148 member countries. The argument put forward by the EU is that trade liberalisation is an important factor in helping to improve the economic and social conditions of many developing countries. This argument also extends to the fact that free trade leads to a more effective use of resources, with only the most efficient producers being successful rather than uncompetitive companies being propped up by tariff barriers. But while at first glance it is evident such an argument has many merits, it is also clear that too much free trade can create unhelpful imbalances that have an impact on the overall security of a nation. For example, while it might be the case that another country can produce food more cheaply, it would not be wise to be completely dependent on that country for food.

TRADE: THE DEVIL IS IN THE DETAIL

Trade negotiations are some of the most complex negotiations that take place anywhere in the world. This is because trade affects all countries and the people that live within them. Trade is a central part of our lives and without trade we would have a very restricted choice of options, from the food that we eat to the clothes and consumer goods that we buy. Trade does, however, come with a health warning. Some people argue that opening up markets for trade is a key vehicle for economic growth and for increasing wealth and prosperity. Others argue that unfettered trade actually results in greater disparity between countries. In the context of the EU, this means that trade policy has to achieve a tricky balance between improving the prosperity and wealth of the EU member states and at the same time helping to improve the prosperity (and stability) of many other countries. To do this the EU has developed a set of policies that both aim to promote trade at a global level while also helping to protect the EU from what are regarded as unfair trading practices.

Because trade agreements impact on such a wide range of countries, companies and individuals, it is no surprise that these negotiations can be subject to a great deal of tension. There are often considerable disagreements between the EU and other countries over market access and the use of subsidies. These relate both to goods being imported into the EU and to the ability of EU companies to secure access to external markets. One of the most long-standing areas of concern has been the subsidies that the EU has provided to a number of industries as a means of support to particular sectors of the economy. Agriculture is the best example of this, where criticism has been levied at the subsidies that the EU pays to farmers via the Common Agricultural Policy (CAP), thereby resulting in accusations of unfairness from non-EU countries. An equally problematic area has been the special relationship that has existed between the EU and the seventy-nine African, Caribbean and Pacific (ACP) countries that enjoy special rights of access to EU markets in light of their status as former colonies of European nations, particularly Belgium, Britain, France and Portugal.

In 1993 a dispute began between the US and the EU over bananas that became the longest-running trade dispute in the history of the WTO. This was despite the fact that neither the US nor the EU actually grew bananas. The background to the dispute was that the EU introduced a new banana import regime that favoured ACP countries rather than producers in Latin America. Mindful of the fact that US companies Chiquita, Del Monte and Dole dominated the production of bananas in Latin America, the US complained that the EU policy contradicted WTO rules as it created a system of inconsistent tariffs. Bananas from the ACP countries were not subject to import taxes while bananas from Latin American countries had to pay taxes. In 1999 the WTO declared the EU policy to be illegal and authorised the US to impose sanctions on the EU to a value of $191 million. The dispute then rumbled on until June 2010 when the EU and the US signed a deal that aimed to end the dispute.

A growing area of concern is the impact that fraud, contraband and counterfeit goods have in the area of trade policy. This ranges from clothing to medicine and Gucci handbags. As with all products, the demand for such goods is subject to market conditions, with recession often resulting in many people being prepared to switch to cheaper goods. Such a decision does, however, come at a price, both in terms of lost revenue to the budgets of the EU and the member state governments as well as health concerns over the standards of the goods. For example, in Britain it has been estimated that at its peak one in five of all cigarettes sold since 2000 have been counterfeit, with many of them being of a low quality that have been smuggled in from China.

The EU and development co-operation

The EU plays a key global role as the largest donor of humanitarian aid in the world, and has co-operative agreements with many

developing countries. In the early years of European integration
the Community's development policy was primarily focused on
the member states' overseas territories and beneficiaries, as the
preamble to the Treaties of Rome contained an obligation for the
Community to create links with former colonies, which became
known as the African, Caribbean and Pacific (ACP) states. In
1963 the Community concluded a trade agreement in Yaoundé,
Cameroon with eighteen former colonies that granted them
privileged rights to export products to the EEC. Thereafter
known as the Yaoundé Convention, it was renegotiated in 1969.

With the expansion of the Community in 1973 to include
Britain there was a need to ensure that a new arrangement covered former British colonies. This led to the signing of the first
Lomé Convention of 1975 (Lomé I). Named after the capital of
Togo, it provided for free trade between what were then the
forty-six members of the ACP states and at that time the nine
member states of the Community. The Convention was subsequently revised. In 1980 a second Lomé Convention, which
increased Community aid and investment, was signed by fifty-
eight ACP states and nine Community member states (Lomé II).
In 1985 a third Lomé Convention, which attached focus to self-
sufficiency and food security, was signed by sixty-five ACP states
and ten Community member states (Lomé III). In 1990 the
fourth Lomé Convention, giving priority to encouraging economic diversification, was signed by seventy ACP states and
twelve member states (Lomé IV).

Although these agreements had assisted ACP states to develop
stronger trading links with the Community, it was also evident
that the relationship had been subject to considerable criticism.
This included the relatively poor levels of economic growth rates
enjoyed by ACP states and the environmental consequences of
prioritising agricultural crops for export. The end result of this
was that a review of the ACP programme started in 1996. This
led to the Cotonou Agreement (named after the capital of Benin)

being signed in 2000 by the then seventy-seven ACP states and fifteen EU member states. A notable difference of the Cotonou Agreement was the considerable focus attached to developing regional organisations among the ACP states, such as the work of the African Union. But while this agreement was designed with the purpose of revitalising the Community's relationship with the ACP states, there remains concern that the seventy-nine ACP nations continue to be influenced by an EU development policy that attaches more importance to symbolism than practice.

The Seventy-nine ACP States

Africa (forty-eight states)		
Angola	Gabon	Niger
Benin	Gambia	Nigeria
Botswana	Ghana	Rwanda
Burkina Faso	Guinea	Sao Tomé and Principe
Burundi	Guinea Bissau	Senegal
Cameroon	Ivory Coast	Seychelles
Cape Verde	Kenya	Sierra Leone
Central African Republic	Lesotho	Somalia
Chad	Liberia	South Africa
Comoros	Madagascar	Sudan
Congo (Brazzaville)	Malawi	Swaziland
Congo (Kinshasa)	Mali	Tanzania
Djibouti	Mauritania	Togo
Equatorial Guinea	Mauritius	Uganda
Eritrea	Mozambique	Zambia
Ethiopia	Namibia	Zimbabwe

Cont'd

Caribbean (sixteen states)		
Antigua and Barbuda	Dominican Republic	St Lucia
Bahamas	Grenada	St Vincent and the Grenadines
Barbados	Guyana	Suriname
Belize	Haiti	Trinidad and Tobago
Cuba	Jamaica	
Dominica	St Kitts and Nevis	
Pacific (fifteen states)		
Cook Islands	Nauru	Solomon Islands
Fiji	Niue	Timor-Leste
Kiribati	Palau	Tonga
Marshall Islands	Papua New Guinea	Tuvalu
Micronesia	Samoa	Vanuatu

In 1992 the EU also established the European Community Humanitarian Office (ECHO) to co-ordinate the EU's response to crises through the provision of such items as foodstuffs, supplies, medical equipment and fuel. This is achieved by ECHO working with partners such as the agencies of the United Nations as well as other non-governmental organisations (NGOs) such as Oxfam and Médecins Sans Frontières, as well as other international bodies. Unfortunately in recent years there has been a succession of crises, which has meant that the EU has become ever more involved in the provision of humanitarian aid. Since 1992 the EU has provided aid to eighty-five countries that have been deemed crisis zones as a result of disasters such as flooding and crop failure. Today the EU is the world's largest donor of humanitarian aid.

For the most part the EU has an established relationship with many poor countries as they require assistance on a regular basis. Some, such as Afghanistan, the Democratic Republic of Congo and Somalia, are regarded as failed states because there is essentially no functioning government. A great number of the world's weakest states are to be found in Africa. Many of these countries border other weak states, which in turn creates a zone of instability. The lack of government in Somalia has led to a lawless country where pirates regularly board and take control of ships passing through neighbouring waters. Aid to these countries is therefore more than just a means of providing food and shelter; it is viewed as an important mechanism in helping to stabilise volatile regions and forms part of a broader EU foreign policy.

In addition to providing humanitarian assistance to countries that are on the 'critical list', the EU also gives aid to other countries such as China and India. This often leads to a great deal of criticism from the European electorate who wonder why we should be providing support to some of the richest countries in the world that have often taken job opportunities away from EU member states. The reality is somewhat more complicated. China might be the second largest economy in the world, but because it is such a vast country the economic wealth per head of population is still very low and as such there are many millions who live in poverty. This is also true for other countries, such as India. Thus, while there is a rationale behind many EU citizens pointing to the poverty in their own member states as being an argument for 'aid starting at home', such a view ignores the fact that foreign aid is a crucial means of providing global stability. We would otherwise live in an even more unbalanced world with greater potential for instability.

Aid is therefore more than just about the provision of foodstuffs and medical assistance. The EU also wants to improve the governance of the countries that it works with, and as such aid is often tied to a broader set of issues that focus on institution building, economic programmes and the promotion of human rights.

Development assistance is complicated by the fact that many of the crises to which the EU responds are man-made. Droughts and crop failure are heavily associated with global warming, the blame for which sits squarely on the developed countries of the world. But as the developing countries expand their economies, this often creates further environmental damage and as such the EU does play an important role in making the argument for reductions in carbon emissions. This often results in EU countries taking the lead because there would otherwise be no reason why poorer countries should reduce their emissions.

Foreign policy

A commitment to develop a collective foreign (and defence) policy has been a recurring theme in the history of European integration. With the Second World War fresh in their minds, Britain and France signed the Dunkirk Treaty in March 1947 to provide a fifty-year alliance to counter the possibility of renewed German aggression. This was superseded by the Brussels Treaty of March 1948, which committed Belgium, Britain, France, Luxembourg and the Netherlands to a system of collective self-defence. In 1949 this European commitment became a transatlantic one with the establishment of the North Atlantic Treaty Organisation (NATO), which from then on became the key bedrock of Europe's defence through the security guarantee that was provided by US membership. But while these Treaties provided a joint security blanket, European member states showed a reluctance to develop the supranationalism that was evident with the creation of the European Coal and Steel Community into defence matters. And it was for this reason that the European Defence Community (EDC) proposal for a common European army failed in 1954. With the failure of the EDC the 1950s and 1960s saw the Community focus on rebuilding the economic and political structures of Europe rather than concentrating on foreign policy and defence issues.

Yet, as the Community's structures became established and as its policies, such as trade, began to develop, it became evident that there was a need for it to establish foreign policy frameworks in relation to how it interacted with the world. This materialised in the 1970 agreement on European Political Co-operation (EPC), which established an informal structure to facilitate foreign policy harmonisation and co-ordination among member states. But while the emphasis that was attached to intergovernmental co-operation ensured that EPC did not encroach on national sovereignty, the absence of an integrated foreign policy meant that the Community was not always able to react in an effective manner to international events.

Pressure for change was initially brought to a head by the ending of the Cold War and the subsequent collapse of the Soviet Union in 1991. The end of the Cold War led many commentators to reappraise established structures and to raise the question whether the EU should take on a stronger foreign and security dimension at a time when there appeared to be less need for US forces to be based in Europe to tackle the threat of a Soviet invasion. In these debates Community member states essentially divided into two groups. First, those who wanted Europe to be able to act alone in security operations. This included Belgium, France, Greece, Italy, Luxembourg and Spain. Second, those who favoured maintaining a close relationship with the US and NATO. This included Britain, Denmark, the Netherlands and Portugal.

In the subsequent two decades that have passed since the Cold War ended, the striking feature is the extent to which the positions of member states have had to adjust to the reality of external pressures and the EU's ability to exercise an independent foreign and security policy. This has come to the fore because, while some commentators suggested that the end of the Cold War would result in a peaceful 'new world order', the reality has been somewhat different, with the post-Cold War period being dominated by a succession of conflicts and wars.

The first test of the post-Cold War order took place in mid-1990 when Iraq invaded Kuwait on 2 August 1990 and resulted in America leading a broad-based coalition of thirty-four states to repel Iraq's invasion in what became known as the 1991 Gulf War. While many European governments contributed to the coalition effort, either through financial aid or through actual forces, for Britain the experience of the Gulf War demonstrated that an integrated, separate, European security and defence identity was unlikely to emerge as Community member states failed to act in a cohesive manner. There was also the reality that the US had the overwhelming military capacity and that Community member states could not match this.

These issues influenced the outcome of the subsequent Treaty on European Union that established an EU Common Foreign and Security Policy (CFSP), but crucially one that was based on member state decision making and did not involve EU institutions. Although this outcome was a classic fudge that satisfied the interests of all member states, in reality it provided the EU with a foreign policy in name only unsupported by resources and infrastructure. This became evident in the 1990s as the EU proved rather feeble in its ability to resolve the crisis that emerged from the dissolution of the former Yugoslavia where civil war resulted in its break-up and the subsequent creation of the new countries of Slovenia, Croatia, Serbia, Macedonia, Montenegro and Bosnia-Herzegovina, while Kosovo was recognised as an autonomous province.

For some commentators, the EU's inability to respond effectively to such tests was summed up by the phrase 'capability–expectations gap', highlighting the differentiation between what

the EU wanted to achieve and what it could achieve. The difficulties here often lay in the fact that the capacity for EU foreign
and security policy was totally dependent on the military
resources being controlled by the member states. But when compared to the US, it was evident that the EU's position as the largest economic market in the world and an equivalent population
did not translate into comparable military resources. Thus, the
EU's international position was often depicted as 'an economic
giant but a military pygmy'.

Partly a response to this situation, the member states agreed in
the 1997 Treaty of Amsterdam to bolster the EU's capacity in
foreign and security policy. This was achieved primarily by the
creation of the post of High Representative, of which the
first incumbent was the former Spanish Foreign Minister and
NATO Secretary-General Javier Solana. But while the Treaty of
Amsterdam also improved the decision-making structure so that
the EU was better able to respond quickly to external challenges,
the overall climate still continued to be dominated by the national
positions of the member states.

Britain and France were the key countries in this debate as they
were the largest EU military powers. Significantly there was a convergence in their viewpoints through the late 1990s. This was
influenced by Britain's realisation that there was a need for a stronger European defence capability, something that was brought into
focus by the crisis in Kosovo at the time. This led to a Franco-
British summit in the French port of Saint-Malo in December
1998 where both countries announced their support for a European
Security and Defence Policy (ESDP). This in turn influenced
member states at the December 1999 Helsinki European Council
to agree on a 'headline goal' of creating by 2003 a European Rapid
Reaction Force of some fifty thousand to sixty thousand with
naval and air support that could be maintained in the field for up
to one year. To facilitate these objectives the EU established the
necessary military committee and support structures.

On 11 September 2001 al-Qaeda terrorist attacks on the US resulted in the collapse of the Twin Towers of the World Trade Center and the destruction of part of the Pentagon. Known thereafter as 9/11, these acts of terrorism emphasised the disorder and conflict that had begun to dominate the post-Cold War world. This viewpoint was summed up by George W. Bush in the US presidential election campaign of 2000: 'When I was coming up, it was a dangerous world, and we knew exactly who the "they" were. It was us versus them and it was clear who "them" was. Today, we're not so sure who the "they" are, but we know they're there.'

While the EU initially provided a galvanised response to the events of 9/11, this quickly began to change when the US took the decision to challenge directly states that harboured terrorist organisations. This led to the preventive war (frequently mis-named a 'pre-emptive war') against Iraq in 2003, which created significant splits within the EU as to the legitimacy of the US-led invasion. While Prime Minister Tony Blair committed Britain to stand 'shoulder-to-shoulder' with the US, other countries, most notably France and Germany, were unwilling to offer such support.

The fallout from the absence of a united EU position was significant, particularly with regard to deterioration in Franco-British relations. This was particularly worrying as their position as the dominant European military powers meant that an effective EU foreign, security and defence policy relied greatly on both their military capabilities. An appreciation of this situation resulted in member states attempting to improve their co-operation through the creation in 2003 of a European Security Strategy, the purpose of which was to emphasise and identify the key threats posed to the EU, namely: organised crime, the proliferation of weapons of mass destruction, terrorism, regional conflict, and failed states. The need for this was subsequently confirmed by terrorist attacks in Madrid on 11 March 2004 resulting in the deaths of 176 people, and in London on 7 July 2005 in which fifty-two people were killed.

But while these terrorist attacks brought to the fore the nature of the security challenges that Europe faces, it was not until the 2009 Treaty of Lisbon that the EU took the decision to establish the post of High Representative for Foreign Affairs and Security Policy, currently held by Baroness Catherine Ashton. This was achieved by amalgamating the positions of EU Commissioner for External Relations with the High Representative for Foreign Policy and was done as part of an effort to provide the EU with a greater clarity and coherence to its external relations policy. The Treaty of Lisbon also established the European External Action Service (EEAS), which came into force on 1 December 2009 and is headed by the High Representative. The EEAS is intended to act as a diplomatic corps that provides coherence both to the administration of the EU's aid and humanitarian budget, but also to co-ordinate the EU's relations with countries around the world. In this sense, the EEAS is a part of a strategy that seeks to deal with the predicament that was raised four decades previously by the former US Secretary of State Henry Kissinger, when he said, 'Who do I call if I want to speak to Europe?'

Upon reflection it is certainly the case that the EU has come a long way since the dilemma that Kissinger highlighted. Since the end of the Cold War the EU has been a more active participant in providing assistance and supporting stability in many of the world's trouble spots. This has ranged from the Balkans to the Middle East, and from Afghanistan to the Congo. A great deal of the EU's efforts have been invested in providing training for the police and judicial services in these countries, with a focus on establishing good governance structures.

What is particularly noticeable about all of the above developments in foreign and security policy is that they have primarily been shaped by external challenges. This has been the key driving force in closing the 'capability–expectations' gap. The creation of the post of High Representative in the Treaty of Amsterdam and the subsequent enhancement of this role in the Treaty of Lisbon were very much focused on bringing greater coherence to EU foreign, security and defence policy. But this is nonetheless an environment that continues to be dominated by the national foreign policies of the member states, which tend to protect their own interests jealously. A direct implication of this has been that the EU continues to have a foreign, security and defence policy that does not reflect its economic strength. This is partly inevitable given the centrality of foreign and defence policy at the national level. But it is also an area where the backlash of the financial crisis that beset nations in 2008 has raised discussions about the need for EU member states to act more closely together so as to trim costs. To this end it is possible that the financial crisis will push member states into being less dogmatic about protecting their own interests.

The EU and the United States

Of all the economic relationships in the world, the one between the EU and the US is the most significant. Together their economies account for approximately half of world GDP and nearly one-third of world trade flows. They also account for the two key international currencies, the euro and the dollar. The transatlantic relationship also has a dominant impact on the global economy because the EU and the US have significant trading and investment activities in other countries and are home to the world's largest multinational corporations. Beyond this economic role, the EU and the US have a substantial political and military impact, given that their military forces are the most powerful in the world and they have extensive international political ties. Many EU countries have strong links with former colonies and this colonial influence also extends to culture and language.

Despite these evident strengths, the relationship between the EU and the US has on many occasions been fraught with tension. The dominant US political, economic and military influence after the Second World War raised concern in many European capitals about American interventionism. This was particularly evident in France, which under the leadership of de Gaulle attempted to keep US influence at bay. But this was very much a double-edged strategy, as French efforts to carve out an independent foreign policy took place within the context of US protection of Western Europe. This protection included the security guarantee provided in the form of NATO. It also extended into the economic field, as evidenced by the financial assistance of the Marshall Plan that provided for the rebuilding of European economies after the war. US support crucially suited American interests as it ensured the stability of Western Europe and thereby provided it with important trading markets as well as a vital buffer zone against Soviet influence during the Cold War.

An inevitable consequence of the close bond between the EU and the US has been the emergence of differences over the years on specific policies. But significantly these differences have rarely done undue damage to the transatlantic relationship. But where tension has occurred, this has highlighted different approaches to world politics. In the 1960s the first notable transatlantic tension centred on the diverse EU and US approaches to the role of NATO as well as the general direction of European integration. This was principally influenced by French concern about US dominance and would lead to NATO's headquarters having to be relocated from France to Belgium. The 1960s and 1970s also saw European governments refusing to provide the US with support in the Vietnam War (1965–75). In the 1970s there were differences between the US and the EU with regard to the foreign policy visions of the Nixon administration, which put particular emphasis on superpower relations. The 1980s witnessed an attempt by the US to reassert its influence at the global level under the Reagan administration, which caused a degree of anxiety among the European public over the deployment of nuclear weapons. The 1990s saw notable differences between the US and the EU over the future direction of the post-Cold War world, including the extent to which the EU should play a leading role. Finally, in the twenty-first century these divisions have continued, especially with regard to the US-led war on terror and divisions between the EU and the US on climate change.

The episodic nature of these tensions has nonetheless provided an impetus for a European response, which has in turn led to the strengthening of EU policies. For example, European Political Co-operation arose from the need to carve out a separate European identity. Its successor, the Common Foreign and Security Policy, was fashioned by a desire to create European capabilities that were independent from US influence. And when these were highlighted as being inadequate at the hands of US intervention in the Balkans, for example, the EU has made further enhancements to its foreign policy capability to rectify this situation.

Of all the areas of tension that have marked EU–US relations in the post-1945 era, the US-led invasion of Iraq has created the biggest impact. While some observers have emphasised that transatlantic divisions were merely an extension of previous differences, others have pointed to the wider ramifications of the EU being confined to the sidelines as the US focuses more on global politics and is less concerned about the intricacies of the transatlantic relationship. For the EU the difficulty is that as the US turns its attention towards developing markets in South America, Africa and Asia, it faces the challenge of both being too weak to be ignored and yet not strong enough to be an equal to the US.

The EU and China

In contrast to the longevity and intensity of EU relations with the US, ties between the EU and China have been a more recent development. Relations were formally established in 1975, with trade agreements being signed in 1978 and 1985. In a stroke this started the process of transforming China from an agrarian, inward-looking country dominated by state control to one that is in many ways the embodiment of free enterprise despite the fact that it continues to be controlled by a one-party Communist government. In the years that have passed the fact that China has the world's largest population has meant that it has emerged as a crucial partner for the EU. An abundance of cheap labour has fuelled China's double-digit economic growth to the extent that it has emerged as the world's second largest economy.

The last two decades, and in particular the period since the millennium, have seen staggering economic growth rates in China. To take one example, whereas in 1977 there were approximately one million cars in the whole of China, by 2009 China had become the largest car market in the world with 13.6 million cars being sold. The end result is that China has become one of the EU's most important trading partners. In recent years EU imports from China have been growing at an average of 18% a year, with the majority of these goods being clothing, textiles, office and telecommunication equipment, machinery and manufactured goods. At the same time China is the EU's fastest growing export market, with the main exports being chemicals, raw materials, transport equipment and agricultural products, which reflects China's status as a developing economy.

The increasing importance attached to these trading relationships has sat side-by-side with EU criticism over China's poor record on human rights and EU concern about the growing assertiveness of Chinese foreign policy at the global level. This includes anxiety at Chinese agreements to secure access to such raw materials as iron and copper from developing countries that are essential for driving the Chinese economy, to concerns about imbalances in global trade towards China. For the EU the difficulty with its relationship with China is that the European economy has grown increasingly dependent on both the importation of cheap products from China and the exportation of higher value goods to China to solve trade imbalances. This has also led to European and American businesses finding themselves increasingly in competition in the Chinese market, and relationships with China are therefore an important context to the wider EU–US transatlantic relationship.

The EU's global role

In reviewing the EU's relationship with the wider world, it is evident that it is an organisation that on the one hand has significant economic strengths that ensure its voice is heard, and on the other suffers from being too weak. The EU's influence is marked by the fact that it is the world's largest economic grouping and also the world's largest trading partner. This in turn results in EU legislation having a significance beyond its borders. Standards prohibiting the use of lead in paint influence toy manufacturers in China. Rules on anti-competitive practices have a profound impact on any company that does business within the EU irrespective of whether the goods are made in the EU. The EU's influence also spreads into the external political and security environment, such as promoting human rights and democracy at the global level. The EU also plays a significant role in improving the lives of many through humanitarian assistance programmes. Increasingly the EU finds itself facing the challenge of dealing with emerging markets and the implications of power shifting in the global economy from West to East. But in this fast-changing landscape, it is also evident that the EU continues to be an important influence at the global level.

11

The European Union: more than the sum of its parts?

Taken as a whole, the significance of the EU cannot be underestimated. It is the world's most successful example of regional integration. It has helped to maintain stability in a region that was previously prone to generating world conflict and has exported stability to neighbouring states through the enlargement of its membership. At a global level the EU's impact is often overlooked. From the provision of humanitarian aid to the training of police officers in developing countries, the EU is the world's most significant organisation for promoting good governance and stability in some of the most lawless countries that exist. It is evident that the EU's influence on world affairs has significantly increased in recent years. One of the most important causes of this has been the process of enlargement. Today the EU has the largest economic market in the world. The GDP of its twenty-seven members is greater than that of the US and over four times that of Japan and Russia.

The process of enlargement has increased the EU's reach in terms of geographical expansion. The EU spreads from Portugal in the West to Bulgaria in the East, and from Finland in the North to Cyprus in the South. Expansion in membership has taken place in recent years at a time when old established orders have broken down with the end of the Cold War. As a result the EU has been faced with having to respond to new pressures and challenges, such as human trafficking, terrorism and the collapse of states, such as Yugoslavia. One consequence of these events is that the EU has had to play a more active role in such areas as the Balkans. Close proximity to the Middle East and Russia has also resulted in the EU having to set out clear policies in these areas. This has ranged from providing humanitarian aid to trying to secure peace and security.

Although the EU's economic and political influence ensures that it is an important power in a modern interconnected world, it is also evident that there are a number of implications from these developments. This includes the extent to which the EU has gained responsibility in areas that are typically viewed as being at the centre of a nation state's remit. The most obvious examples of these are trade, security and defence policy, and a single currency. Such developments raise several pertinent points about the extent to which the EU can now be viewed in the same way as nation states who have traditionally been the main actors in foreign affairs.

The EU's claim to statehood is weakened by the fact that its influence is heavily dependent on the role of the member states to enforce its policies. The EU itself has relatively little in the way of financial resources when compared to the member states. Many people do not consider themselves to be 'European' in terms of their citizenship. This is despite the fact that more and more people work and travel in other member states. The latest statistics also show that 13% of marriages in the EU take place between citizens of different member states. For some countries notions such as European citizenship are more problematic than others. In Britain it is rare to find public buildings flying the European flag, while Europe Day celebrations barely register among the public.

Looking to the future, it is apparent that many EU member states are undergoing a process of dramatic transformation in the organisation of the services that are undertaken by the state.

From Dublin to London and Athens to Madrid, governments are establishing policy objectives that are defined by an age of austerity shaped by the 2008 international financial crisis and subsequent eurozone crisis.

The eurozone crisis is without doubt the greatest challenge that the EU has faced since the end of the Second World War. It has demonstrated the complexity of uniting economies of differing strengths. It has also exposed fundamental weaknesses in European economies that have developed bloated budget deficits. This has resulted in the need for significant economic restructuring, including the creation of a fiscal union in the eurozone to support monetary union. But more than anything else, the crisis has highlighted a shift in global power towards China and India as well as such emerging economic dynamos as Brazil. The EU may have the largest single market in the world, but it has struggled to control an economic emergency that has spread from one member state to another.

Inevitably a key question emanating from the eurozone crisis is what impact it will have on the EU's future. In the first instance, it is evident that despite the doomsayer predictions that the eurozone crisis has heralded the end of the EU, it is unthinkable to consider that the EU or the euro will not survive. Rather, the constrained financial resources of member states will actually create pressure for governments to work closer together to solve their common problems. These vary from responding to terrorist threats to competing with China.

Thus, whatever concerns the public have about European integration, the likelihood is that more and more areas of national life will become Europeanised in the future. But rather than viewing this as an erosion of national sovereignty, what we are essentially talking about is shared sovereignty. In other words, member states do not give up their sovereignty to some amorphous organisation. The member states are after all the EU itself. In practical terms, this means that member states will have to make more and more use of the EU institutions, such as the Commission and the Court of Justice, to protect their own national interests.

Just as we can expect a greater extent of shared decision making at an EU level, we can also expect that there will be further changes to the way that the EU is governed. At present the EU is governed by institutions that suffer from weak legitimacy. This particularly applies to the European Parliament where there continues to be a development lag between the augmentation of its powers and its weak legitimacy. This is in part a product of low turnout in European elections, which in turn points to the fact that the European Parliament does not operate in a manner that citizens would expect. European elections are not about the choices of what the EU should be about, as they are basically just a focus for the electorate to express their discontent with national governments. But the Parliament has also been timid in using its powers to reinforce democracy.

Going forward there needs to be a serious debate about European ideas to establish a consensus about the EU. And this is, of course, important in the context that shared sovereignty is likely to increase. The political vacuum that currently exists within the EU at the level of the institutions could equally be applied to the national level where member state governments have rarely engaged in a full and frank debate about the EU. It is a situation that is not helped by a move to technocratic governments in Greece and Italy in 2011. To this end, it is this need to open up a debate about the EU, including the opportunities and constraints of membership, that is the greatest challenge the EU and its member states face in the years ahead.

Further reading

Websites

European Union: www.europa.eu.int
European Commission Delegation to the United States:
    www.eurunion.org
University Association for Contemporary European Studies:
    www.uaces.org
European Community Studies Association: www.ecsanet.org
Centre for European Policy Studies: www.ceps.be/index.php
The Federal Trust: www.fedtrust.co.uk
Royal Institute of International Affairs: www.chathamhouse.org.uk

Introductory studies

Archer, C. 2008. *The European Union.* Abingdon: Routledge.
Blair, A. 2010. *European Union since 1945*, 2nd edition. Harlow: Longman.
McCormick, J. 2008. *Understanding the European Union*, 4th edition. Basingstoke: Palgrave.
Pinder, J. 2007. *The European Union: A Very Short Introduction*, 2nd edition. Oxford: Oxford University Press.
Warleigh-Lack, A. 2009. *European Union: The Basics*, 2nd edition. London: Routledge.

Comprehensive textbooks

Bache, I. & George, S. 2009. *Politics in the European Union*, 3rd edition. Oxford: Oxford University Press.

Bulmer, S. & Lequesne, C. 2012. *The Member States of the European Union*, 2nd edition. Oxford: Oxford University Press.

Cini, M. & Pérez-Solórzano Borragán, N. eds. 2009. *European Union Politics*, 3rd edition. Oxford: Oxford University Press.

Dinan, D. 2010. *Ever Closer Union: An Introduction to the European Union*, 4th edition. Basingstoke: Palgrave.

Egan, N., Nugent, N. & Paterson, W.E. 2009. *Research Agendas in EU Studies: Stalking the Elephant*. Basingstoke: Palgrave.

McCormick, J. 2011. *European Union Politics*. Basingstoke: Palgrave.

Nugent, N. 2010. *The Government and Politics of the European Union*, 7th edition. Basingstoke: Palgrave.

Historical development

Dinan, D. 2010. *Europe Recast: A History of European Union*. Basingstoke: Palgrave.

Dinan, D. ed. 2006. *Origins and Evolution of the European Union*. Oxford: Oxford University Press.

Milward, A. 1999. *The European Rescue of the Nation State*, 2nd edition. London: Routledge.

Pinder, J. 1998. *The Building of the European Union*. Oxford: Oxford University Press.

EU institutions

Alter, K. 2009. *The European Court's Political Power*. Oxford: Oxford University Press.

Arnull, A. 2006. *The European Union and its Court of Justice*, 2nd edition. Oxford: Oxford University Press.

Corbett, R., Jacobs, F. & Shackleton, M. 2011. *The European Parliament*, 8th edition. London: John Harper.

Hayes-Renshaw, F. & Wallace, H. 2006. *The Council of Ministers*, 2nd edition. Basingstoke: Palgrave.

Hix, S. & Høyland, B. 2011. *The Political System of the European Union*, 3rd edition. Basingstoke: Palgrave.

Judge, D. & Earnshaw, D. 2008. *The European Parliament*, 2nd edition. Basingstoke: Palgrave.

Nugent, N. 2000. *The European Commission*. Basingstoke: Palgrave.

Peterson, J. & Shackleton, M. eds. 2006. *The Institutions of the European Union*, 2nd edition. Oxford: Oxford University Press.

Spence, D. & Edwards. G. eds. 2006. *The European Commission*, 3rd edition. London: John Harper.

EU policies

Geddes, A. 2008. *Immigration and European Integration: Towards fortress Europe*, 2nd edition. Manchester: Manchester University Press.

de Grauwe, P. 2009. *The Economics of Monetary Union*, 8th edition. Oxford: Oxford University Press.

Hantrais, L. 2007. *Social Policy in the European Union*, 3rd edition. Basingstoke: Palgrave.

Hill, C. & Smith, M. 2005. *International Relations and the European Union*. Oxford: Oxford University Press.

McCormick, J. 2007. *The European Superpower*. Basingstoke: Palgrave.

Sjursen, H. ed. 2006. *Questioning EU Enlargement: Europe in Search of Identity* London: Routledge.

Vogler, J., Whitman, R. & Bretherton, C. 2010. *The External Policies of the European Union*. Basingstoke: Palgrave.

Wallace, H., Pollack, M.A. & Young, A.R. eds. 2010. *Policy-Making in the European Union*, 6th edition. Oxford: Oxford University Press, 2010.

Europe and the world

Hill, C. & Smith, M. 2011. *International Relations and the European Union*, 2nd edition. Oxford: Oxford University Press.

Leonard, M. 2005. *Why Europe Will Run the 21st Century*. London: Fourth Estate.

Meunier, S. 2007. *Trading Voices: the European Union in International Commercial Negotiations.* Princeton: Princeton University Press.

Rifkin, J. 2004. *The European Dream.* Oxford: Polity Press.

Smith, K. 2008. *European Union Foreign Policy in a Changing World.* Oxford: Polity Press.

Index

The following abbreviations are used in the index:
ECJ = European Court of Justice
EP = European Parliament.
Page numbers in bold indicate chapters or main sections.